HOW TO
PAINT YOUR
TRACTOR

Tharran E. Gaines

Voyageur Press

First published in 2009 by MBI Publishing Company and Voyageur Press, an imprint of MBI Publishing Company, 400 First Avenue North, Suite 300, Minneapolis, MN 55401 USA

The information in this book is true and complete to the best of our knowledge. All recommendations are made without any guarantee on the part of the author or Publisher, who also disclaims any liability incurred in connection with the use of this data or specific details.

We recognize, further, that some words, model names, and designations mentioned herein are the property of the trademark holder. We use them for identification purposes only. This is not an official publication.

Voyageur Press titles are also available at discounts in bulk quantity for industrial or sales-promotional use. For details write to Special Sales Manager at MBI Publishing Company, 400 First Avenue North, Suite 300, Minneapolis, MN 55401 USA.

To find out more about our books, visit us online at www.voyageurpress.com.

Library of Congress Cataloging-in-Publication Data

Gaines, Tharran E., 1950-
  How to paint your tractor / Tharran E. Gaines.
     p. cm.
  Includes index.
  ISBN 978-0-7603-2861-3 (sb : alk. paper)
  1. Protective coatings. 2. Farm tractors--Conservation and restoration--Handbooks, manuals, etc. 3. Farm tractors--Painting. 4. Sheet-metal--Painting. I. Title.
  TS698.G36 2009
  629.28'7--dc22
                                    2008042976

Editor: Leah Noel
Designer: Greg Nettles
Cover Designer: idesign, inc

Printed in Singapore

On the front cover
A freshly painted Farmall Cub exits the shed where it was restored. *Lee Klancher*

On the frontis
A crisp paint job and a restored emblem really bring this Oliver tractor back to life.

On the title pages, main
When applying a coat of paint, you can avoid putting excess paint on one side of the pattern while producing light spots on the other side by holding the gun perpendicular to the surface being painted.

On the title pages, inset
With the introduction of its New Generation line of tractors, John Deere also introduced a new shade of green paint, known as Agricultural Green, on its models. *Chester Peterson Jr.*

Contents

Acknowledgments

As has been the case with every book on classic tractor restoration that I have written, I could not have gathered all the necessary photos and information without the help of a large group of people. Even though I don't have any antique tractors myself, and have a limited amount of experience working on tractors, I have approached tractor restoration in much the same way I did when I was a technical writer for companies like Sundstrand, Hesston, Winnebago, and Kinze. My job with those companies was to glean information from a variety of sources in marketing, engineering, product service, and the test lab and turn it into manuals that could be used by the customer to assemble, service, or repair the machine he or she had purchased from my employer.

I figure the people I have talked to and photographed while preparing this book have forgotten more than I could ever learn about classic tractor restoration and painting. So, in reality, this book is their story, not mine. With that in mind, I want to express my sincere appreciation to a couple people in particular. One of them is Jim Deardorff, owner of Superior Coatings in Chillicothe, Missouri. Although he has done more than his share of tractor painting, Jim's real specialty is media blasting. In addition to stripping the paint off of everything from classic tractors and cars to a vintage jet, he has also had articles on the subject published in several trade publications.

I also owe a debt of gratitude to Gary Ledford, a paint technician from St. Joseph, Missouri, for his help on the chapters regarding paint and primer selection and application.

Others who have provided resources, illustrations, or information include Jim Seward, from Wellman, Iowa; Paul Cummings, from Amsterdam, Missouri;

Gilbert Vust, from Portage la Prairie, Manitoba; Larry Karg, from Hutchinson, Minnesota; Jeff Gravert, a tractor restorer from Central City, Nebraska; Tom Armstrong, owner of N-Complete in Wilkinson, Indiana; Dallas Mercer, owner of Mercer Restoration in Excelsior Springs, Missouri; O'Reilly Auto Parts in Savannah, Missouri; Jerry Schmutzler, a tractor enthusiast from St. Joseph, Missouri; Reynolds Collision and Alignment in Savannah, Missouri; B. J. Rosmolen, owner of BJ's Auto Collision and Restoration in St. Joseph, Missouri; Chris and Kim Pratt, who write and edit the *Yesterday's Tractors* online magazine found at www.ytmag.com; Walter Bieri, a Farmall collector from Savannah, Missouri, and Estel Theis, a John Deere two-cylinder collector who is also from Savannah, Missouri. I also received help and information concerning decals from a number of decal suppliers (see Appendix B), including Travis Jorde, Lyle Wacker, Lyle and Helen Dumont, and Gaylen and Eugene Mohr.

I'm sure there are people who I have forgotten, and, if so, I apologize. Still, I sincerely appreciate the help from each and every person who has contributed along the way.

Most of all, though, I want to thank two women for their extreme patience with me as I kept them waiting time and again. One is my wife, Barb, who has not only blessed me with her encouragement, but has spent several hours proofreading the copy and the photo captions for typographical and grammatical errors. The other is Leah Noel with Voyageur Press for her editorial guidance and direction on this project, not to mention her extreme tolerance every time I asked for an extended deadline. She and her boss, Michael Dregni, have been a pleasure to work with over the past several years.

Introduction

You don't have to talk to very many people who have painted tractors to learn that preparing to paint is generally more important than the actual paint job. Over and over, they'll tell you that the best way to ensure a beautiful tractor is to make sure the sheet metal is as smooth as you can get it and that it has been properly cleaned and prepared before you ever apply that first coat of primer.

By the same token, no tractor painting project is complete until all the decals and/or emblems have been replaced and the serial number plate has been buffed, polished, or sanded.

Consequently, even though the title of this book refers to painting tractors, it's important that all the bases are covered. That means starting with cleaning and sheetmetal preparation, choosing and applying the correct primer, applying the appropriate paint type, and finishing off your labor of love with a clean set of decals.

Finally, it's important to note that you will often see the words "restoration" or "tractor restorers" mentioned in this book. That's because most tractor painting jobs are done in conjunction with a complete tractor restoration. Thanks to the growing interest in tractor shows and classic tractor collecting,

Those who restore tractors for a collection are continuously looking for something unique, like this Ford 9N orchard model. It's especially hard to find orchard models like this with good sheet metal.

each year a growing number of people take on the challenge of hunting down a collectible or nostalgic tractor model and restoring it to like-new condition. Of course, that means painting it to look as good as or better than it did when it was driven off the dealer's lot.

Even if you hire a graphic artist to customize a pulling tractor with unique scenes, you'll still need a solid coat of paint as a base for the tractor.

On the other hand, a number of hobby farmers and property owners simply want to fix up a good work tractor for mowing or loader work. Many times, the tractor is in pretty good condition but just looks a little worse for wear. So a paint job, along with a good tune-up, seems to be in order. The same goes for some farmers who simply want to keep their equipment looking good.

As the interest in vintage tractors has grown, so has the appeal for implements to go with them. Consequently, you may eventually find yourself painting more than a tractor.

CHAPTER 1

UNDERSTANDING THE BASICS

Although the process of painting a tractor may have a lot of similarities to the way your local auto repair shop or body shop paints a car, you'll find that there are also a lot of differences. Most obvious, perhaps, is the fact that with few exceptions, all models from any particular tractor manufacturer are painted the same color. That color may have changed over the years, as you'll discover later; however, in most cases, when a farmer selected a brand, he got a red, green, blue, or orange tractor, no matter the model.

One exception was a series of tractors introduced by the White Farm Equipment Company in 1989. As a way of commemorating the three brands that had been merged to form the White tractor brand, the company offered the White American model in the customer's choice of Minneapolis-Moline yellow, Oliver green, Cockshutt red, or White silver. That is one of the few models in tractor history that ever came in a choice of colors.

If you're familiar with tractor history, you also know that most early-day tractors were a little like Henry Ford's Model T, which only came in black. Any

One difference between painting an automobile and a tractor is that, with few exceptions, all tractors of a particular brand and time period are painted the same color.

In the early days of tractor production, most tractors were painted a dark or dull color, ranging from gray to dark blue and dark green.

tractor purchased in the early part of the twentieth century, or prior to the mid-1930s, was usually dark green, gray, or dark blue. Once one company adopted bright colors, though, they all seemed to follow.

Unfortunately, unlike automobiles, tractors don't have a tag or decal on the frame that tells you the correct paint color. Granted, all late-model Allis-Chalmers tractors are orange and late-model Oliver tractors are green. The shades of colors changed over the years, however, and it's been left to the collectors and tractor restorers to come up with the appropriate paint codes to match. Figuring out which paint color is correct falls back to consulting the serial number plate, which can be used to find out what year the tractor was built. Then, it's a matter of referencing Chapter 9 or other tractor resource books

Allis-Chalmers was one of the first manufacturers to introduce a tractor model with brighter-colored paint. It is believed that the president of Allis-Chalmers selected orange after seeing a field of poppies in bloom.

Rare tractors like this one built by the Avery Company, which folded before World War II, naturally hold more value when restored. However, locating parts for them can be a treasure hunt. *Hans Halberstadt*

to tell you what year color changes occurred so you can determine the correct shade.

Paint Type

It seems the paint chemistry employed by tractor companies often lagged behind that used by the automotive industry. In most cases, early-day tractor manufacturers used lacquer paint topped off with a few water-transfer decals. Of course, one of the things that made lacquer the choice of previous generations is the reason you seldom see it used anymore—its solvent evaporates quickly.

On the plus side, quick drying time allows imperfections to be rubbed out easily and repainted almost immediately. It does, however, require multiple coats of paint to attain coverage. Also, because of lacquer's rapid solvent evaporation, the Environmental Protection Agency discourages its use. And, to be honest, few people do use it, partly because lacquer paints for tractors are hard to find.

According to paint specialists, lacquer has other disadvantages, including the fact that it dries to a dull finish and must be buffed to bring out a shine. Lacquers are the most photochemically reactive, too, which means they fade over time when exposed to sunlight. Finally, lacquers do not withstand exposure to fuel spills and chemicals, as well as other types of finishes. That's part of the reason old tractors have such a dull appearance after so many years of wear.

Naturally, improving technology eventually led the farm equipment industry to switch to enamel paints, which continue to be used today. In the meantime, the automotive industry has moved on to urethane coatings and base-coat/clear-coat systems.

Most vintage tractors were originally painted with lacquer paint, which not only is prone to fading, but lacquer coatings are totally incompatible with today's enamel paints.

Paint Chemistry

Whether you're talking about lacquer, enamel, urethane, or latex house paint, all coatings have one thing in common: Each type consists of three to four main ingredients. These include pigment, binder, thinner or solvent, and, as is often the case with newer formulations, additives. According to paint specialists with Van Sickle Paint, the color comes primarily from the pigment, which also serves to provide coverage and protect the binder from weathering.

The binder, meanwhile, acts as the vehicle that carries the pigment as it is being applied and holds the pigment together when it's in the dry film form. The type of binder used also determines the durability of the end product and provides adhesion to the surface to which it is applied. It's usually the binder, in fact, that determines the type of paint and how it's used. Each is unique in the type of benefits it provides.

Linseed oil, for example, is used as a binder in exterior applications only and is primarily used on wood surfaces as a preservative. Alkyds are also used as binders and can be used in both interior and exterior applications. When it comes to tractor and automotive paints, most products use one of two binders that produce a tough, weather-resistant coating. Oil-based acrylics—not to be confused with acrylic house paints—are used almost exclusively for exterior paint coatings, since they produce a flexible, yet versatile, coating. Polyurethane is another binder that produces a tough paint coat. For that reason, polyurethane is most often used in automotive coatings and in products used on concrete.

The solvent or thinner is combined with the pigment and the binder to control the consistency; however, it can also play a role in the film-drying characteristics. Finally, the additives can play a wide range of roles, particularly with today's chemistry. They can aid in pigment dispersion, help control the application properties, and help some product formulations dry quicker or more evenly.

So how does paint really dry? Again, that varies with the formulation. As mentioned earlier, lacquers dry through evaporation of the solvent. Others, such as linseed oils, dry through oxidation and polymerization. Latex paints, such as those used on exterior and interior home surfaces, dry through evaporation of water and fusion.

Although some individuals like to restore vintage tractors for their collections, others simply want a restored and repainted tractor for use as a work tractor.

When it comes to the type of paints used on automobiles, tractors, and industrial applications, though, you're looking at products that dry as they're chemically catalyzed.

Volatile Organic Compounds

As was explained earlier, paint formulations usually contain some type of solvent or thinner that evaporates during the drying and curing process. These vapors, as well as any chemical substances that enter the atmosphere during the painting process, are referred to as volatile organic compounds (VOCs). These compounds don't just come from paint, though. They can originate from any noxious chemical, including formaldehyde, benzene, and xylene, which can trigger short-term headaches, dizziness, and nausea. Besides being emitted by paint, they also come from cleaners, glues, plastics, caulk, carpeting, and pressed wood products. Due to the vast number of sources in today's petrochemical society, several states, including California and New York, have already passed laws that regulate the emission of VOCs.

As a result, paint companies are already working on lowering the VOCs in their products. In fact, you'll probably get used to seeing "no VOC" or "low VOC content" on many products you'll use. The use of new products, such as the high-volume low-pressure (HVLP) spray paint systems, will also play a role in your safety, not to mention paint quality. Not only do HVLP systems provide better accuracy, but because they don't require as much pressure, there's less overspray and less paint bounces off of the surface being painted.

Quality Comes at a Price

When it comes time to purchase the paint for your tractor, you'll find that there is a wide range in price. In fact, you can pay anywhere from $10 a quart to more than $100 per quart. Obviously, the price will vary a great deal, depending upon the type, as illustrated later in the chapter on choosing the right paint. The new automotive-type finishes and urethane coatings are going to be a lot more expensive than acrylic enamels, and the latter are going to be more expensive than the implement enamel sold at the local farm supply dealership.

Other factors that influence the price of paint include the amount of hiding pigment in the formulation versus the amount of filler pigment, the quantity and quality of the resin or binder used in the product, and the additives that provide special performance or improve application. Some of the more expensive paint formulations, for example, contain additives that make the coating less prone to fading when exposed to sunlight for long periods of time.

Compatibility

Pick up any book on painting a car, and it will probably include a section about scratch repair or repainting a damaged panel. Unfortunately, that isn't as easily done with a tractor, unless you're touching up the paint on a fairly new model.

As was previously mentioned, most older tractors were painted with lacquer, which is totally incompatible with today's enamel and urethane coatings. One way to see what type of paint was previously used is to put a little lacquer thinner on a clean, white cloth and rub it on a hidden area of the tractor. If the tractor was last painted with lacquer, you should be able to see color on the cloth after some firm rubbing. If it has been repainted with enamel, however, or it had a coat of enamel as the original coating, some color will come off immediately, and the paint on the treated area should begin to wrinkle.

Naturally, the same thing would happen if you were to put enamel over the top of the lacquer in an attempt to repaint or touch up the finish. The only way you can apply a new coating is to strip the sheet metal or casting down to bare metal and apply a primer coat or clean the metal of all loose paint and rust, apply a sealer primer, and put on one or more coats of new paint.

As you'll learn later in this book, all the products you use during the painting process must also be compatible, not only with the surface being painted, but with each of the other products in the paint system. In other words, you probably don't want to mix PPG hardener with DuPont paint or rely on an off-the-shelf reducer to thin your John Deere enamel, even though a number of painters have successfully mixed brands. It's kind of like Russian roulette. Sometimes, you'll get along fine. Other times, the unfortunate tractor restorer has watched the paint coat start to wrinkle. It's up to you whether you want to take the chance.

You'll need to plan on applying several thin coats of paint, as well. One thick coat may provide adequate coverage, but a single, thick coat can lead to many problems. When paint is applied too thick, it can lead to wrinkling, surface skinning, and cracking, not to mention slow drying and stress that can cause premature failure. Even in multiple layers, automotive paint produces a much thinner coating than something like house paint. That means any blemishes are going to show up much more readily than if you were putting a coat of house paint over siding that had simply been scraped prior to painting.

With all of that said, it's time to start removing parts and preparing the surface. After all, surface preparation is the single *most important* variable in determining the service life and appearance of any paint coating. Even the best paint or most expensive coating will not adhere to an excessively dirty or greasy surface, or if moisture and contaminants get beneath the paint film.

It's important that all the paint products you are using, including primers, paint, thinners, and hardeners, are compatible. While this "off" brand may be fine for some paint types, it may not be for others. You'll find that professional body shops usually use materials made by a single manufacturer to ensure compatibility and prevent unexpected problems.

During the preparation process, you'll also need to repair or patch any dents, tears, and rust spots on the tractor. And rest assured, there are bound to be several. Farm tractors are and always have been the most important work tool on the farm, and as such, they get used pretty hard and treated poorly at times.

Consequently, you'll find techniques in the following chapters for repairing minor and major sheetmetal damage, and for replacing components. If the surface isn't perfectly smooth, all the defects will certainly show up in the paint coat. And if the cast iron and sheet metal aren't at least covered with a sealer prior to painting, the paint will fill any voids left behind in the surface, resulting in a dull, uneven finish.

CHAPTER 2

SETTING UP SHOP: TOOLS AND FACILITIES

If you're serious about doing a first-class tractor restoration or paint job, the first thing you're going to need is a good set of basic tools to remove parts such as the shields, fuel tank and radiator. Make sure you put the emphasis on *good*. Cheap tools are only going to lead to frustration as they break, strip, or worse, damage a tractor part. Look for a set of automotive-quality tools that come with a warranty, such as those offered by Sears (Craftsman), NAPA, and Snap-On.

You'll want to start with a drive socket set that contains sockets ranging from 1/16 inch to 1 inch. In addition to a ratchet handle, you'll need a breaker bar to loosen stubborn bolts without risking damage to the ratchet. A set of combination wrenches will come in handy, too. There are some places on your tractor that you simply can't get a socket and ratchet into.

Since the sheet metal and a number of components will have to be removed before painting a tractor, you will need a good set of basic tools that includes wrenches, pliers, screwdrivers, and more.

Paul Cummings of Amsterdam, Missouri, not only has his tools conveniently arranged, but they also are in a cabinet that can be locked.

A cutoff tool or band saw will also come in handy if your restoration requires much metal work.

You may or may not need a welder during your restoration project. But even if you do, you can probably find a friend to help you out or take the piece to a commercial welder.

You can decide which will work best for you and your budget, but choices include open-end, box-end, and wrenches that provide an open-end configuration on one end and a box-end of the same size on the other. To round out your tool collection, you'll want to add a couple of adjustable wrenches (often referred to as crescent wrenches, even though Crescent also is a brand name), a full set of regular and Phillips screwdrivers, a pair of adjustable pliers, needle-nose pliers, and a pair of locking pliers (often referred to by the popular brand-name Vise-Grip). In fact, if you plan to do much sheetmetal work, you may want two or three pairs of locking pliers to clamp and hold parts in place for welding. Vise-Grip-type pliers are available in a variety of shapes and configurations. They're also infinitely adjustable within their applicable range and can be attached and removed with just one hand.

Other tools that you may need at some point or another include a good hacksaw, a punch set, and a cold chisel. And don't forget to pick up a couple of putty knives. You'll need those for scraping away grease and grime.

Don't assume you have to go out and buy all new tools. Due to the economy and changes in agriculture, farm auctions are far too common these days. So keep your eyes open for an estate sale or a shop liquidation where you can pick up what you need at a reduced price.

Body Tools

If you're going to be doing any sheetmetal repair— and chances are you'll find it necessary—you'll need a few basic body repair tools. The truth is that it's pretty rare to find a tractor that doesn't have at least a few dents or ripples in the hood, grille, or one or both fenders.

In most cases, you can get by with a simple body hammer and dolly. Although body hammers and dollies both come in various sizes and shapes, the role of the hammer is to stretch and shape sheet metal, while the dolly acts as the anvil to keep it from moving too far.

Since most shops have a ball-peen hammer in their inventory, you might find that of value as the body hammer, too, since one end of the head is rounded and the other end is flat. The key is to hold the dolly on the back side of the dent or crease while striking the front side.

Another tool that may be valuable in certain situations is a dent puller, though these are generally used in areas where it is hard to gain access to the back side of a dent. In essence, this is a slide-hammer device that is attached to a hole drilled into a dented panel and used to pull it back into place. The drawback is that the holes you make to attach

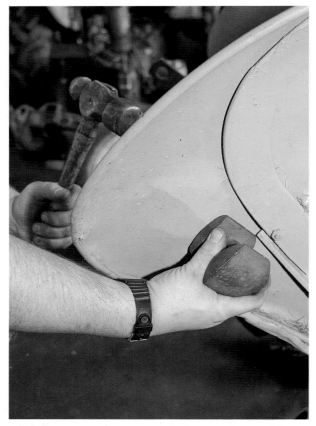

Although body hammers for sheetmetal work are available in a wide variety, you can generally handle most repairs with a multipurpose body hammer and a handheld anvil or a ball-peen hammer and a metal block for backup.

the slide hammer to the sheet metal have to be filled later with body putty. As a result, it's generally better to remove the panel, grille, or fender and simply use a hammer and dolly.

If the sheetmetal component is one that you can remove and relocate to a more solid location, you may even want to invest in some kind of an anvil. You don't have to run out and spend hundreds of dollars for a commercial shop anvil, though. For what you'll need most of the time, a 2- or 2½-foot piece of railroad track rail will do. In fact, the rounded edge of the rail will work better than a real anvil for some sheetmetal repair and fabrication.

If you occasionally need a flat surface or a square end for bending, you can weld a piece of bar stock across one or both ends of the rail so it will stand upright when turned rail side down.

Hoists and Jacks

Depending on how much work you're doing to the tractor, you may need equipment to lift and support the unit or other components, particularly if you remove the wheels for painting. Consequently, you'll need some heavy-duty lifting equipment capable of raising the tractor to the level where you can block it up on stands or wooden blocks. Don't try to get by with concrete blocks! They can crumble or crack too easily, posing a physical danger. Don't try to pile blocks up too high, either. One option is to build cribbing under the frame, which means you place strong wooden blocks log-cabin style under the tractor or axles as structural support until the wheels can be safely reinstalled.

Your lifting and cribbing needs will depend, too, on the tractor model you're restoring. Basically, there are two types of tractors. One type has a rail or cast-iron frame that extends from the front of the tractor to as far back as the rear axles. The engine, transmission, and other components are then mounted inside the frame. With this type of design, engine work and other types of repair can be done by simply lifting the engine or transmission out of the frame.

Other kinds of tractors use the engine and transmission as load-bearing components. All Ford

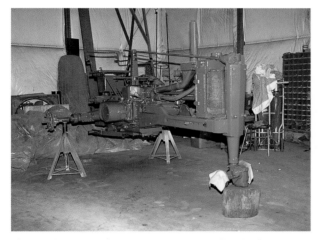

If you plan to remove the tires and wheels during the painting process—which generally works best—you'll need a set of jacks or some type of cribbing to hold up the frame.

Not everyone has the luxury of having a hoist available in an area that's large enough to serve the needs of both a tractor overhaul and painting project.

tractors, for example, use this design. However, you'll find some brands that use both configurations, depending on the model. If you're doing any other work on this type of tractor design, you'll need a support of some type to hold up the two halves as you split the unit. This is unnecessary, of course, for painting a tractor, but you'll need to keep it in mind if you intend to do any repairs while you have the sheet metal and hood removed; otherwise, the need for jacks and hoists will pretty much be limited to something sufficient to raise the unit while you remove the wheels.

Just be sure you keep safety in mind and you have the right equipment to do the job. For example,

don't try to lift the rear end of the tractor with a single bottle jack, even if it is an eight-ton jack. That's not what you would call adequate stability.

Grinders, Sanders, and Files

Depending on the amount of bodywork you have to do on the sheet metal before painting, you're going to need some type of grinder, sander, or both. A grinder can't generally be used for light sanding or buffing because it spins too fast. But if you get the right model, it can be used for an assortment of jobs—including grinding down welds where you've had to make a splice, cutting out rust areas, and smoothing rough spots. Equipped with a wire

An angle grinder can be a valuable asset for sheetmetal work and for grinding down any welds required as part of the repair process. Equipped with a wire brush, it also works well for removing loose paint.

Some grinders are designed to perform double-duty as a sander and polisher, too. Of course, one of the most useful tools for bodywork is a dual-action (DA) sander (above) that works in two different ways to provide a smooth, swirl-free finish.

You probably already have some type of sander that will work for removing paint, sanding body putty, and more. You just need to make sure it can handle the wide variety of sandpaper grades that you'll need to finish your project.

Quite often, an automotive paint store will have as many as or more sandpaper choices than a hardware store, particularly when it comes to texture ranging from course to very fine grades needed for finish work. These are all designed for use with a DA sander.

brush, it can also be used for rust or old paint removal. And by substituting a sanding disc for the grinding wheel, you can do some rough shaping.

Grinders basically come in two types: electric or air-driven. Both have advantages and disadvantages. Air tools are generally lighter weight and less bulky, but you need to have an adequate air compressor.

On the other hand, it's often easier to drag around an extension cord than a 1/2-inch hose. Also, electric grinders come in different sizes, making them more adaptable to your needs.

Another thing to consider is that if your needs are limited, a good electric drill may be sufficient. You can find a wide assortment of tools to fit a 3/8-inch drill, including grinding discs, wire brushes, and sanding discs. Plus, you'll probably need a drill at some point anyway.

You won't be able to get along without a good sander, though. Again, several types are available, including both air- and electric-powered units. Both types can be found as disc sanders, orbital sanders, straight-line sanders, and belt sanders. Perhaps the most popular among those who do a lot of painting and bodywork are the air-powered dual-action (DA) sanders. Because of their dual action, which prevents scratches and swirls from forming, they work equally well for rapid shaping of body filler and fine finishing work.

Disc sanders also work well for feathering paint and body filler, and they can be useful for buffing when equipped with a buffing pad. But you need to watch out for swirls if they're used on a fine finish. The same goes for straight-line sanders, which work great for removing old paint and working large plastic-filled surfaces. They can, however, leave distinct scratch marks that will have to be sanded out before painting.

Finally, an orbital sander works great for smoothing body filler on both vertical and horizontal planes, particularly since orbital sanders generally have a large sanding pad; however, these still won't leave the smooth, swirl-free finish that a DA sander is capable of producing.

Unfortunately, you'll probably need a few tools powered by elbow grease and a little wrist action, as

Regardless of how much mechanized sanding you're able to do, you'll still need to use a sanding block at times.

This sponge sanding block not only features a fine grit for finish sanding, but it has a trapezoid shape that allows you to get into creases and edges.

well. Among these are a metal file to clean and shape sheetmetal panels and a Surform or "cheese grater" file for shaping body filler. The latter isn't used on metal, but instead it has an open-tooth design that allows it to shave off filler material before it hardens. It's possible you already have one of these because they're also used to shape wood.

Last but not least, you may want to keep one or more sanding blocks on hand for hand sanding tight spots. One thing I have found to be very handy are the small, wet sanding blocks that are made from a sponge rubber. Since the sanding grit is adhered to the rubber face on four of the six sides, they easily shape to the surface contour. Plus, when the grit gets clogged, they can simply be rinsed in a bucket of water, squeezed out, and reused again and again.

Air Compressor

While an air-powered sander can be a valuable asset when removing stubborn rust and paint, air-powered tools aren't quite as necessary as the air compressor itself. Its most obvious use, of course, is to power the paint sprayer; however, an air hose and nozzle are also invaluable for blowing dust and dirt out of crevices and away from parts while you're cleaning surfaces. If you're doing a full tractor restoration, you'll want to use it to blow out fuel lines, water passages, and the like. It will also come in handy when you get to engine repairs.

Most commercial body shops use a compressor with at least 10 horsepower. For the average tractor restorer, however, a compressor rated at 5 horsepower or greater is generally sufficient. The goal is

One of the key pieces of equipment for tractor painting is an air compressor with adequate capacity. You'll find compressed air equally helpful when cleaning surfaces and components before you start spraying paint.

to have a compressor that can build up a reserve of compressed air in the tank and then shut off for a few minutes to cool down.

If the compressor works too hard and doesn't have a chance to shut off, the friction generated will increase the air temperature, which, in turn, leads to condensation in the air lines. And moisture in the air supply doesn't go well with acrylic- and urethane-based paints.

Tank Volume

You'll need to consider the volume of the air tank on the compressor, too. Generally, this goes hand in hand with the horsepower level of the compressor and is set accordingly by the manufacturer. If the tank doesn't have enough capacity and the pump can't keep up, you're going to be painting a few minutes, stopping to let the air supply build in the tank, then painting a few more minutes, and then waiting again.

The best way to determine the volume you'll need in the air compressor is to find out the cubic feet per minute (cfm) of air required by your spray gun and consult the application guide sheet for the paint product you intend to use. You might, therefore, want to shop for a paint sprayer before you look for a compressor.

Air Pressure

The final criterion concerning the compressor is air pressure. The gauge may say one thing, but you need to make sure the air pressure at the paint gun meets the minimum psi rating specified on the product label or in the product's application guide.

Even if the pump has the capacity to produce the appropriate amount of pressure, it can easily be lost if the air has to travel too far through too small of a hose. In general, most paint specialists recommend the hose have at least a 5/16-inch inside diameter. Even then, 60 pounds of pressure can drop by 6 pounds over 25 feet of 5/16-inch hose length. In comparison, the same 60 pounds of pressure can drop by 19 pounds when traveling through 25 feet of 1/4-inch hose.

For HVLP spray guns, it pays to go larger, which means that 3/8-inch hose is generally recommended.

You'll need plenty of air hose to move around the tractor while painting. However, keep in mind that the greater the distance, the greater the air pressure loss. Most paint specialists recommend the hose have at least a 5/16-inch inside diameter to prevent excessive pressure loss.

Regardless of what type of compressor you use, you'll need some type of air filter, since raw air contains small but harmful quantities of water, oil, dirt, and other contaminants that can affect the quality of the sprayed finish.

Regardless of the size of the hose, you need to select the ideal compromise. In other words, you want enough hose to be able to freely move around the tractor, but not so much that it results in a loss of air pressure over the required distance.

Air Filter

No matter what type of compressor you own or purchase, you need to realize that raw air contains small but harmful quantities of water, oil, dirt, and other contaminants that can affect the quality of the sprayed finish. This may not have been a problem if you only used the compressor in the past to power air tools or inflate tires, but it's different when you use a paint sprayer. Air filters filter out these contaminants before they get on your paint job. Air entering the filter is swirled to remove moisture that collects in the baffled quiet zone. Accumulated liquid is then carried away through either a manual or automatic drain.

Most paint gun and air tool suppliers will have a variety of filters and filter systems that will work for your application and budget.

It's important to have a quality paint gun that you feel comfortable using. That's why a lot of tractor hobbyists continue to use a conventional siphon-type paint gun.

Your local paint supplier will have a variety of paint guns available, including complete kits that have everything you need but the air hose.

Paint Guns

Since this book is about painting tractors, perhaps the most important piece of equipment you'll need is the paint gun. Before you decide to purchase one, you'll need to do a little research and evaluate your needs. Some restorers still use a siphon-type gun that siphons the paint out of a canister or cup and draws it into the air stream; however, a growing number of serious tractor restorers have switched to an HVLP (high-volume low-pressure) unit, even though the gun costs about twice as much as a siphon unit. Regardless of the type, the role of the paint gun is to use air pressure to atomize a sprayable material like primer or paint onto a prepared surface. In the paragraphs that follow is some more information on your options.

Conventional Spray Guns

Although they have pretty much been abandoned by the automotive world, conventional spray guns are still used with great success by a number of people who paint tractors. Obviously, a conventional siphon-type gun is going to be your lowest-priced option. The greatest drawback is that they typically require 60 pounds of air pressure or more to work properly.

That means the paint is also hitting the surface at a much higher pressure and more of the product is being atomized into the air. Consequently, by some estimates, as much as 65 to 70 percent of the paint can be wasted as overspray. In addition, the greater amount of air pressure is more likely to stir up dirt and debris that can land back on the

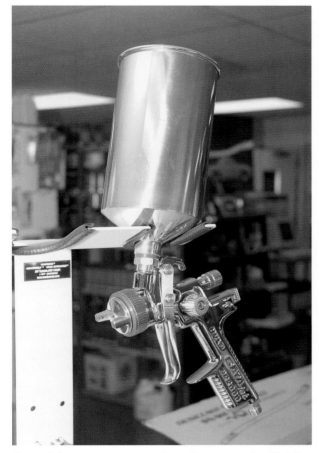

One of the newest types of applicators is the HVLP, or high-volume, low-pressure paint gun, which helps conserve paint and reduce vaporization.

Some of the newer HVLP guns even offer the option of using them with a canister as a siphon gun or with a paint pot as a pressure-feed gun.

fresh paint coat. If you're one who prefers a conventional gun, however, don't worry. Some of the reputable companies known for their HVLP guns, such as DeVilbiss and Sharpe, still make a very good siphon gun, too.

High-Volume Low-Pressure (HVLP) Spray Guns

Basically, a high-volume low-pressure spray gun is just what the name implies. It works by increasing the volume of paint passing through the nozzle, yet it requires substantially less pressure at the nozzle. That doesn't mean it requires less air pressure from the air compressor, though. The important thing is it uses less pressure to propel the paint from the gun, which means less waste. Consequently, if you

plan to do a lot of painting, you may want to consider an HVLP gun, knowing that the savings in quality paint can offset the cost difference in two or three uses.

An HVLP gun is also better for the environment, not to mention friendlier to your shop or work area, since the amount of overspray is substantially reduced.

HVLP guns can be divided into two primary categories: pressure feed and gravity feed. Since the use of pressure-feed guns is pretty much limited to body shops and professional painters, your most likely choice will be a gravity-feed gun, although there are a few companies that market a siphon HVLP gun. This type of gun has the paint cup mounted above

You'll find that your paint dealer has plenty of accessories for painting, too, including this Dirt Pic for removing stray contaminants from wet paint.

the air nozzle so paint feeds directly into the airstream by gravity. This design further contributes to the need for less air pressure, although you may need to refill the cup more often than you would a siphon-gun canister.

Additional Paint Gun Considerations

No matter what kind of paint gun you buy, it's important that you get a quality unit. The old adage that you get what you pay for is still true in this case. A cheap gun is likely to produce cheap-looking results. Consequently, it's generally best to purchase the gun at a reputable paint supplier or auto supply store. You not only stand a better chance of getting a quality gun, but the sales staff can explain the gun's operation and the best way to care for it. Plus, they can do a better job of matching the gun to the type of paint you plan to use and the type of surface you're painting.

Jim Deardorff, owner of Superior Coatings in Chillicothe, Missouri, also advises restoration enthusiasts to check into the price of replacement parts. A reasonably priced spray gun may not be that good of a deal if the replacement nozzles are exceptionally expensive, or, at the very least, if they are just as costly as they are for a higher-quality gun.

Finally, you'll want a gun that is fairly easy to clean and take care of, since it's important to clean the gun after each use. Paint guns require very small air and material passageways in order to atomize the paint. As a result, the guns can easily clog if paint is allowed to dry in small orifices or if debris infiltrates the passageways.

Although the manual that came with your paint gun should provide the best procedure for cleaning the unit, you should know that cleaning it basically involves rinsing the paint cup with solvent to remove the bulk of the paint or primer, then filling the cup with the prescribed amount of solvent and spraying it through the unit. Quite often a second round of solvent is recommended to ensure that the gun has been thoroughly cleared and only clear solvent comes out the nozzle.

You may also want to acquire a spray gun cleaning kit that includes the appropriate brushes for cleaning the housing, air caps, and other ports. Just be sure you don't use any sharp objects or a piece of wire to try to clean any ports or nozzles. It takes a precision instrument to take 30 to 40 pounds of air pressure and use it to push a one-millimeter drop of paint through a nozzle into an eight-inch pattern. If you damage the nozzle, you've damaged the gun's ability to do its job. And don't soak the whole gun in solvent thinking that "if a little is good, a lot is better." The solvent can loosen debris on the outside and allow it to enter passages it wouldn't have gotten to on its own.

Finish up by blowing clean air through the gun to remove any remaining solvent from the passageways and wiping down the gun with a clean cloth that's been dampened with a small amount of solvent.

Work Area

If you're doing a complete tractor restoration, chances are you already have a shop or garage available. That doesn't mean you have to do all the work inside, though. In fact, it might be a good idea to move outside when stripping paint or using a wire brush to remove rust and grime. Thanks to the fresh air, you won't be exposed to as many fumes or dust particles. It would be best, however, if you can work

While your work area doesn't have to be anything fancy, it does help to have a place where you can keep the tractor indoors while it is being disassembled, especially when it comes time to paint the tractor.

on a concrete pad so it's easier to clean up the residue and debris.

On the other hand, it gets pretty hard to move a tractor once you've started disassembling the unit or removed the wheels. Once you've pulled off the hood and fuel tank, it's pretty hard to get the tractor started. So you may want to find an area where you can do everything from rebuilding the engine, if necessary as part of the restoration, to applying the paint.

At some point, however, you'll need to make preparations in order to maintain some manner of cleanliness. In the section about paint guns, the problems of paint mist and fogging were discussed, yet bodywork can be pretty messy, too. All that dust you create when sanding body filler is going to settle somewhere. Suffice to say, a good exhaust fan will help draw a lot of material out of the air, but you should also remove as much other equipment as possible just to keep it clean.

Next, get some large plastic sheets or painter's drop cloths to cover tools, workbenches, storage

As a retired farmer, Estel Theis of Savannah, Missouri, still has a well-equipped shop that serves as a site for restoration projects during much of the year.

shelves, etc. Keeping things covered will save you a lot of cleanup later.

Jim Seward, a tractor painter from Iowa, says he likes to make a "paint booth" around the project with a drop cloth or plastic sheeting. The plastic not only keeps paint from drifting away from the

Your paint area should also have some kind of exhaust ventilation fan or a way to move fresh air through the area without introducing dust and debris.

area, but the plastic holds enough static electricity to attract dust and spray that could negatively affect the paint coat.

Some painters also recommend that you wet down the floor prior to doing any painting, including the application of primer. Naturally, it helps if the floor is clean to begin with so you don't end up with mud. The idea is that it minimizes the risk of stirring up dust that can end up embedded in the paint; however, you certainly don't want to overdo it if you do wet down the floor. For one thing, it increases the electrocution hazard of working with electrical devices. It can also increase the humidity in the work area, which can create new problems.

Next, take a look at your lighting. It certainly helps to have good lighting while performing other work, like engine repair or bodywork, but it's even more important when painting. You need to be able to see how the spray is going on and whether an area has been sufficiently covered, which will help avoid touch-ups later. One of the easiest solutions is to set up a four-foot fluorescent light fixture like those commonly available at hardware and home improvement stores. You might even be able to build a unit that can be moved around the tractor as you paint.

Finally, you really should have some sort of storage area or cabinet that can be locked or secured. Paint and the other chemical products that you will be using can be very dangerous. If they're not toxic, they're at least flammable and should be kept out of the hands of anyone not intent on using them properly.

A respirator approved for use with organic mists is one of the most important pieces of equipment to have on hand when painting a tractor. Remember, too, that not only are paint fumes hazardous to your health, but they are flammable.

Safety Equipment

Selecting the right paint and equipment for tractor restoration and painting is one thing. Gathering the right equipment to protect yourself while performing a quality job is quite another. In the long run, the latter is really the most important. At the least, your protective equipment should include rubber gloves, protective clothing, and an approved respirator or mask.

To be safe, use a respirator approved for organic mists, which is the type labeled for use with pesticides. A charcoal-filter mask may be sufficient for enamel paint, but not for urethane coatings and acrylic enamels to which a hardener has been added. These contain chemicals known as isocyanates, which are especially toxic. Therefore, the use of urethane requires either a fresh-air mask and painting suit, or a charcoal-filtered mask, hat, gloves, and a fully ventilated environment. That's because isocyanates are not only dangerous when inhaled, but they can be absorbed through body pores and the tear ducts in your eyes.

Don't just wear your mask when painting either. Granted, paint products are most dangerous when they have been atomized by the paint gun, but the paint dust you generate when you're sanding dried paint is just as bad. So keep a filtered mask on any time you're removing old paint or rust, shaping body filler, or sanding new paint.

CHAPTER 3

DISASSEMBLY

One of the first things you'll need to do if you want to do a quality job of painting your tractor is to remove as much of the sheet metal as possible. That includes the fenders, fuel tank, grille, hood, and so on. If you're painting the tractor as part of a restoration, you may have already removed these parts to work on the engine, transmission, or cooling system.

Regardless of when it's done, removing the sheet metal is important for a couple of reasons. First, unlike an automobile, which has most of the frame and engine hidden under the body, tractors have most of the frame, engine, and even the transmission exposed. In the majority of cases, they're also painted the same color as the sheet metal; however, it's pretty much impossible to paint the frame or the powertrain components without removing most of the sheet metal first.

Secondly, many tractor restorers like to treat various parts of the tractor differently. That applies to the sheet metal, frame, cast components, and engine. Some parts, for example, can be sandblasted—or media blasted, as they call it now—to clean them up. Other parts need to be treated with much more care.

The first thing you'll need to do when preparing a tractor for painting is to remove all the sheet metal.

Judging from all the rust on this vintage Oliver tractor, it's going to take some work to get the sheet metal, engine, and frame cleaned up enough to paint.

The same is true for this old Ford 8N, which at least appears to be complete and in good shape.

While disassembling the tractor, make note of any missing parts that need to be replaced. Farmall restorers warn that you need to make sure the cover plate that provides access to the cultivator steering mounts isn't missing, as is the case with this tractor. They can be costly to replace.

Even if you are one who chooses to media blast both the frame and the sheet metal, you certainly won't want to use the same type of media on both.

There are differences, too, in the types of primer you'll want to use on the sheet metal and cast components. More on that later. Needless to say, an enamel primer may be fine for the frame, while the sheet metal may need a filler primer to smooth out any remaining blemishes.

Finally, some people even like to use different types of paint on the sheet metal and frame. While some simply use the same enamel on the entire tractor, others like to paint the engine, frame, and cast components with enamel and then finish off the hood, fenders, and remaining sheet metal with a urethane, or a base coat and clear coat. Hopefully, the information in this book will help you make your own decisions about the latter.

Take Your Time

Before you start pulling parts off the tractor, it's important that you evaluate the situation and take your time, labeling parts, if necessary, as you go so you'll know how they fit back together. Keep a pad and pencil handy for recording measurements and taking notes. Used in combination with a service manual, the notes and images you record today will be a valuable resource later on.

Before you start removing paint, you should also take note of any original decals that are still left

While disassembling the tractor and cleaning parts, make a list of other parts that are beyond repair so you'll have time to search parts sources and swap meets for them.

The first thing you might want to do before removing the sheet metal and stripping the paint on a vintage tractor like this vintage Oliver is to make notes on its decal locations.

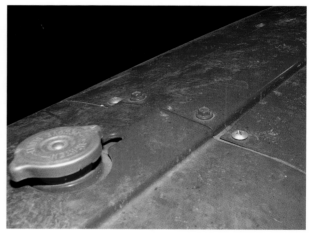

You'll find that most sheetmetal parts are held on with screws or bolts and nuts, as is the case with the Farmall and Case tractors shown.

on the tractor. Grab a tape measure and a notebook and record the position of each decal. You might note, for example, that the "L" on your Farmall decal should be positioned six inches back from the seam where the hood and grille meet, or the bottom of the "brand" decal is 1½ inches from the bottom edge of the hood piece.

You may want to take some photographs in the process to use for reference later on, when it's time to apply new decals. You'll want some good photos anyway, if for no other reason than to show your friends what the tractor looked like before you started.

As you start disassembling the tractor and removing sheet metal, you'll notice that most joints and attachments still use traditional bolts, nuts, and washers or screws as fasteners. So you'll need a good set of hand tools that includes wrenches, a set of screwdrivers, and a good set of pliers. You'll also need a systematic way to keep the pieces from getting lost or broken before the paint has dried and it's time to reassemble the tractor. One way to organize them is

Part of the hood on some tractors, such as the one on this Farmall, is held in place with metal clips so it's easier to remove for engine service. Removing the grille and fenders will involve a little more work.

to collect a bunch of egg cartons and put the nuts and bolts from different areas into individual egg compartments. You can even use and label separate egg cartons for different parts of the tractor (i.e., one for the grille and hood, one for the fuel tanks). For bigger bolts or parts, you can use coffee cans or plastic butter tubs.

It's worth noting, too, that it's often impossible to simply remove the sheet metal before taking a few other important steps. As an example, on several early-model John Deere tractors, it's necessary to disconnect and completely remove the steering shaft before you can remove the hood, since it passes through a hole in the hood. The same procedure applies on a few International-Harvester Farmall models.

In fact, this type of configuration has led to a few problems that still plague tractor restorers today.

On some tractors—particularly early John Deere two-cylinder models—the steering shaft passes through the hood. That means you'll need to disconnect the steering assembly and remove the shaft before you can remove the hood.

Go ahead and remove any emblems or nameplates while you're removing the sheet metal. They'll need to come off before stripping the paint anyway. You'll find that most are held on by screws, nuts on the back of the panel, or clips.

Again, the early John Deere A and B models are a good example. Not only do you need to remove the steering shaft to remove the hood, but it's necessary to remove the hood in order to remove the muffler. For early-day farmers who were in a hurry to get back to the field, this often proved to be too much time-consuming effort; hence, they simply cut out a hole around the muffler to reach the bolts hidden underneath. If that was the case on your tractor, you'll need to patch the hole as part of the restoration process prior to painting. See Chapter 5 for more information on that process.

Finally, some tractors have an insignia, nameplate, or logo attached to the front of the grille. Some of the Farmall tractors, such as the 400 or 560, also had metal numbers and nameplates on the side of the tractor. In each case, these will need to be removed prior to prepping the sheet metal for painting. In most cases, these emblems or nameplates are held on with small nuts and washers that attach to a threaded shaft, or they're held on with clips that pinch onto a stud on the back of the emblem. Whatever the system, use care not to strip anything if you plan to reuse the piece. In most instances, you can get a new or reproduction replacement, should you choose to do so. The truth is that it's pretty hard to make a scratched, dull hood emblem look good on a nice glossy paint finish.

Use a Gentle Hand

Whatever you do during disassembly, don't throw anything away while you're removing parts and gaining access to the frame. Even if a piece is rusted beyond any possible use, it may be needed as a pattern for creating or purchasing a new piece later on.

Finally, be careful about using too much force when trying to remove rusted or frozen parts. In your haste to break things loose, it's easy to damage irreplaceable parts, especially if you're restoring a classic farm tractor. Quite often, the best bet is to use a combination of penetrating oil, patience, and a properly sized tool.

If the part can withstand the heat, a propane or oxyacetylene torch and occasional taps with a hammer can be as effective as anything. Alternately

John Deere collector Estel Theis of Savannah, Missouri, found that the fenders on a vintage John Deere Model D he purchased were beyond restoration. However, he needed to hang on to them for a while so he could copy the bolt pattern onto the reproduction fenders that have since been mounted and painted (background). In the meantime, the best original one still makes a good "table" for work materials.

using heat and penetrating oil can also be helpful. Just don't apply oil to hot metal or direct an open flame toward a pool of penetrating oil. Be careful, too, about using a torch on a part where the heat can be transferred to a bearing. Unless you know you're going to be replacing the bearing or part during a complete restoration, the time you save may not be worth the cost.

Today's tractor restorers are fortunate that a wide variety of sheetmetal components is available from aftermarket sources. These components include fenders, hoods, battery boxes, and grilles.

Remove or Mask?

As you're disassembling the tractor, you'll find plenty of other little pieces that need to either be removed or masked with tape before cleaning or painting. These include items like the steering wheel, gearshift knob or other rubber-handled knobs, rubber seat springs, and hydraulic hoses and fittings. Unless it's a late-model tractor, on which the steering wheel is all plastic or composite, you'll need to paint the spokes along with the rest of the tractor. That can often be more easily done when the steering wheel is removed from the tractor.

You'll find that most older tractors have a steering wheel composed of hard rubber molded around the outer rim of the steering wheel. Unfortunately, it often becomes cracked over time, leaving you with a couple of choices. You can either send it off to have it repaired or purchase material for patching it yourself. That will be covered in a later chapter.

You'll normally find that the gearshift knob is either screwed onto the shaft or press fitted onto ribs on the end of the shaft.

As for the need to remove hydraulic hoses, that depends a lot on the age of the tractor. Most tractors didn't include a hydraulic system until the 1930s at the earliest. Even then, it was often an internal system, which was the case with the Ford 9N, 2N, 8N, and NAA models. If there are external hydraulic hoses on the tractor, they should be removed and the fittings plugged with a standard pipe plug. For one thing, the hoses will need to be cleaned and degreased, but you'll also need to be able to get to the surface beneath the hoses for cleaning and painting.

You'll need to decide, too, how you're going to handle the gauges. If you're planning to replace or refurbish them, it's generally best to simply remove the gauges now. Most of the time, they're held in place on the back side of the instrument panel by

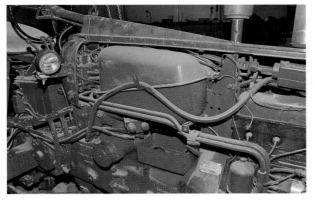

Once you get the sheet metal off, you can move on to removing anything that shouldn't be painted, such as the fuel sediment bowl or filters. On some tractors, the distributor should remain unpainted, as well. With most tractors, it's also helpful to remove the fuel tank in order to reach the area underneath it. The fuel tank can always be painted separately.

a bracket and a couple of nuts and washers. If you don't plan to do anything with them, however, it's important that you carefully mask them with several layers of tape to protect the glass and bezel that hold them in place.

Other components that may or may not need to be removed before painting will be covered in the chapters that cover sheetmetal preparation, paint stripping, masking, etc. Needless to say, you can use your own judgment as you look over the tractor. When you remove the hood, for example, you'll see the obvious need to also remove the battery and battery cables, the fuel filter with its glass bowl, the glass jar found on many air filters, belts, hoses, and the like.

Finally, you'll find that some tractors, including many Farmall and John Deere tractors built from the 1930s through the 1950s, often included a screen in the grille. Unless it's in good condition and it is painted the same color as the rest of the grille, you'll want to remove that, too. At the very least, you'll want to repaint it with the rest of the tractor. But if it is dented, torn, or gouged—which is usually the case if the tractor has seen many years of use— you may just want to find a replacement screen and paint it as a new piece.

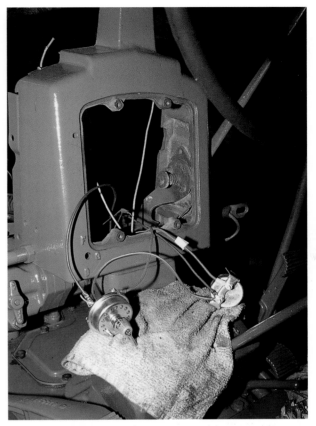

It usually works best to remove the entire dash or instrument panel before painting. First remove the gauges and switches, and then paint the panel as a separate unit.

A Ford 8N tractor being restored by Chris Mercer and his father, Dallas Mercer, has been completely disassembled and is ready for paint preparation. *Dallas Mercer*

CHAPTER 4

SURFACE CLEANING AND PREPARATION

Without a doubt, surface preparation is the single most important variable in determining the life of any paint coating, whether you're painting your house or a vintage tractor. Even the best paint you can buy won't adhere to an excessively dirty or greasy surface or if moisture and contaminants get behind the paint film. So the first step you'll need to take with any tractor is getting it clean.

You may have cleaned the tractor to some extent already. If you bought the tractor at a sale, there's a good chance the previous owner even cleaned it up to make a good impression with prospective customers. Or you may have run it through the car wash on your way home.

Once you've removed the sheet metal, it will become obvious how much grease has accumulated on the engine, frame, and transmission.

Regardless of how much cleaning has been done to this point, though, the job has really just begun. The sheet metal will need to be thoroughly cleaned and degreased. And once the sheet metal has been removed, you're bound to find a lot more grease and grime than was originally evident.

The goal is to make sure every surface will hold the primer and paint you will be applying later. To handle tough, baked-on grease on the engine, frame, and powertrain, some restorers like to spray oven cleaner on the really greasy areas and let it soak before power washing the whole tractor. Others use a hand-pump sprayer to soak the tractor and engine with diesel fuel for several hours.

It is not recommended that you use gasoline or kerosene as a cleaner. The cleaners and degreasers available at any automotive store are both safer and more effective. In the meantime, you might even want to keep a putty knife, screwdriver, and wire brush handy while you're cleaning to dig at the really caked-on stuff.

Jim Deardorff, owner of Superior Coatings in Chillicothe, Missouri, insists that even if you plan on sandblasting the frame and drivetrain, it's important that you first remove as much grease as possible. Hitting it with a sandblaster, he insists, will only drive grease particles into the surface. That is especially true if you use too much pressure or the type of media that can pit or scratch the surface. If grease is driven into the pits or scratches instead of removed, it will only make it more difficult to apply a quality paint job. As a result, Deardorff uses a combination of stripper and media blasting on most cast-iron components.

Before he does that, though, he uses a hand sprayer to apply a coat of Dawn dishwashing detergent over the entire tractor and lets it soak overnight. It's not that Deardorff specifically endorses Dawn, but it's the only detergent he has found that rinses clean without leaving any kind of film. Don't dilute it with water, he cautions, or it will foam too much. If he uses anything to thin the Dawn concentrate, Deardorff will add 10 percent to 20 percent of a product called Chlor*Wash (see Appendix B), which is a multipurpose cleaner formulated to

In the early stages of tractor cleanup, a putty knife and wire brush can be valuable tools for removing baked-on grease, particularly on cast-iron surfaces. In this case, cleaning up the tractor was combined with a brake replacement job.

remove dirt and salts that can cause corrosion. In fact, Deardorff says Chlor*Wash also works well for cleaning restored tractors that have been exposed to exhaust fumes, salts, and dirt during tractor shows and events.

Once the detergent or combination has had 10 to 12 hours to soak, Deardorff uses a power washer and hot water to completely clean the project. If that isn't enough to remove the majority of the grease, he occasionally picks up the oven cleaner.

Cast-Iron Preparation

In most cases, the easiest way to finish preparing steel and cast-iron components, once you've gotten most of the grease off, is to use a sandblaster or hire

Sandblasting, or media blasting, is perhaps the quickest way to remove paint and rust from cast parts and heavy components, such as the wheels and frames.

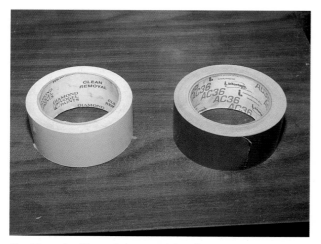

Jim Deardorff masks everything he wants to protect during media blasting with a layer of masking tape covered by a layer of duct tape.

someone to sandblast the components for you. This includes the frame, wheels, transmission, and rear-end housing.

Before you start any sandblasting, it's vital that you go over the entire tractor, looking for holes that will let sand in and cause later damage. Many machines have passages to the brakes in the pinion housings. Be sure to pack these areas with heavy rags. Check, too, to see if any of the bolts you removed during disassembly left an open hole that will let sand into the clutch or shaft areas. If so, you'll want to put bolts back in these holes.

Unless you're planning to replace the spark plugs on a gasoline engine, it's a good idea to pull the good spark plugs and replace them with old plugs or dummies. At the very least, you'll want to remove the spark plug wires and cover the entire distributor to protect the distributor cap. The same goes for the coil. If the distributor body and shaft are to be painted, some restorers simply remove the cap and rotor and mask off the top of the distributor itself.

Watch out for the clutch inspection plate, as well. It won't seal well enough to keep sand out. Most water pumps also have a vent on the bottom side that will let sand up into the bearing and shaft area. Don't count on just trying to avoid these areas, because if there is a hole, sand will get in.

Don't rely on masking tape to adequately protect an area either. With enough pressure behind it, sand will go right through masking tape. Instead, some restorers rely on multiple layers of duct tape placed over any vulnerable components or openings.

Jim Deardorff says he likes to use masking tape covered by a layer of duct tape. Masking tape by itself isn't enough, he insists. On the other hand, media blasting material can tear up the plastic backing on the duct tape, making it very difficult to remove when you're finished. A layer of masking tape beneath it solves this problem.

Deardorff has another tip for those who find themselves masking off a hydraulic cylinder shaft prior to sandblasting or painting. While very few older tractors included hydraulic cylinders, you'll still find them on tractor loaders and on some of the three-point lift systems.

If you plan to sandblast the tractor frame, don't forget to cover the serial number plate with several layers of duct tape to protect it from damage.

Although this John Deere two-cylinder tractor has extensive fire damage, the sheet metal appears to be in good condition.

"If you have a cylinder shaft that you need to mask off, simply run a piece of heavy fishing line along the length of the shaft before wrapping it with tape," he says. "Then, when it comes time to remove the tape, you can just pull on the fishing line and 'unzip' the tape."

The radiator can also pose a challenge when it comes to sandblasting the tractor frame. In most cases, the best bet is to simply remove it from the tractor. If there is any area on the frame that really needs cleaning, it's probably the area under the radiator anyway. That's where the rust, caked-on dirt, and grease are prone to collect in the first place. So if you don't remove the radiator, you're going to miss a vital area.

If by chance you don't remove the radiator prior to media blasting, you should at least cover the radiator core with several layers of cardboard and seal the seams with several layers of duct tape. That is unless you plan to replace the whole radiator core anyway.

Be sure you cover the serial number plate, as well. Depending upon the age of your tractor and the serial number, this can be a valuable component, especially if you're painting an older, vintage tractor. Wheels and cast parts can be sandblasted without much risk of damage. In fact, if you're dealing with spoke wheels, sandblasting may be the best way to get in and around the individual spokes.

The last method of removing paint, and the one you're probably going to have to employ as well, is mechanical removal. Unfortunately, this method requires the most sweat and hard work. You'll find a wide range of items available at most hardware and automotive stores for this task, but you might want to start with the basics, including wire brushes and putty knives. A wire brush or a sander that fits on an electric drill can also come in handy when removing paint and grease from powertrain and frame components.

Sheet Metal

Thanks to the huge interest in antique tractor restoration, today's tractor restoration enthusiast has more choices than ever before. Due to the growing interest in the restoration hobby, vendors now offer hundreds of sheetmetal parts as aftermarket reproductions. Leaf through any issue of an *Antique Power*, *Red Power*, or *Green* magazine and you'll find ads for everything from complete bare-metal hoods to replacement fenders, dash panels, grilles, and PTO shields. If you're working on a vintage Ford tractor, N-Complete and Carpenter both offer reproductions of nearly any sheetmetal component you could ever need, including fenders, hoods, and nose pieces for 8N, 2N, and 9N models.

In addition, plenty of sheetmetal parts are available through salvage operations that specialize in

You'll find that some tractor hoods have a ridge on the underside that was originally meant to provide strength and rigidity. Unfortunately, ridges that fold inward easily collect moisture and dirt, which can cause the hood to rust from the inside out. By the time it gets to this point, as illustrated on a Ford 8N hood, it's often too late for body filler. You may want to save your time and effort and just purchase a replacement.

Because the grille on styled farm tractors is easily dented or gouged, it is often damaged beyond simple repair. Even the optional bumper failed to fully protect the grille on this Ford 9N. Replacement grilles are often available at a reasonable price.

vintage tractors. Finally, a number of businesses, including many tractor dealerships, sell what is commonly referred to as new-old stock (NOS). These are old parts that have never been used, but instead have been stored in a warehouse or stock room and have only recently been "discovered" and put into circulation to meet the growing demand from antique tractor enthusiasts. Unfortunately, due to the number of tractor brand mergers in recent years, these are becoming harder to find; however, there's still a potential to find such parts within the John Deere, Case IH, and AGCO dealer networks.

Repair or Replace a Sheetmetal Component?

If you've discovered a significant amount of sheet-metal damage on your tractor, you may want to consider the options before going much further. If you choose to keep the original piece, you're still going to have to remove the old paint and then make the appropriate repairs before it is usable. As a result, you may be thinking that if a new hood or fender is available, as mentioned in the previous section, you could be further ahead just by buying a new one. So consider the following factors that play into such a decision:

First of all, is there a replacement component available for your tractor brand and model? You certainly won't find any for vintage tractors like a Twin City or Hart-Parr model. And they're not made for "orphan" tractors like a Silver King or Friday model. Orphan tractors are those that were built for only a short time by companies that no longer exist or weren't acquired by another company as part of a merger. Replacement parts are available, though, for some of the most popular brands like Ford, John Deere, and Farmall.

Where is the damage located? Near the edge or right in the center? Is it on a flat portion of the hood or on the curve?

How bad is the damage? Are the edges torn and gouged or is it rusted through? How hard will it be to return it to its original shape?

Can the component be easily removed and relocated to an area where it is easier to work on? Will it need to be welded?

How much time do you have available to make the repair? And do you have the experience—i.e., if welding is required—to make the repair?

How does the cost of a new fender or hood, for example, compare to that of taking the part to a professional for patching?

All of these things need to be considered before you take on sheetmetal repair or place an order for the new hood. And there's nothing to say you can't compromise and have a professional weld in a patch, leaving you to do the body filler repairs and preparation. On the other hand, it's true that time is money. At the time of this book's publication, a replacement clamshell fender for a John Deere Model A, B, 50, 60, 70, 620, 630, 720, or 730 was listed at $129 plus postage. A flat-top fender was $215. Similarly, the fender panel for a Ford 9N, 2N, or 8N without the mounting bracket and no Ford script was listed for $79.

So the choice is really yours. If the satisfaction of restoring the old piece is worth more than $100 to $200, go for it.

Sheetmetal Paint Removal

Due to the availability of so many new parts, some restorers like to replace any sheetmetal parts that are in questionable shape with reproduction components. For others, particularly those on a tight budget, it's more economical to strip and repair existing sheetmetal components, unless they are extremely rusted or wrinkled. Whatever route you take, it's important to get as much paint as possible off the sheet metal. At the very least, you'll want every bit of loose paint off the parts, but new paint and primer will always adhere best to bare metal.

Media Blasting Sheet Metal

When it comes to using a sandblaster or media blaster to strip sheet metal, you'll find differing opinions. Some restorers sandblast all the sheet metal and every bit of the frame prior to a restoration project. Others wouldn't take a sandblast nozzle anywhere near the sheet metal, regardless of how much elbow grease it saved.

The key word here is "sandblasting." These days, it's more commonly referred to as media blasting,

Media blasting makes quick work of paint removal on the wheels of this classic John Deere two-cylinder tractor.

simply because there are a lot more media types than sand that can be used. That's particularly the case when you're media blasting sheet metal. Check out current media suppliers and you'll find a wide variety of media types, including aluminum oxide, garnet, glass beads, plastic beads, wheat starch, carbon dioxide pellets, and even dry ice.

Jim Seward, a tractor restorer from Wellman, Iowa, who also manages the body shop for a local General Motors dealership, is one who uses a sandblaster on everything. He insists sandblasting sheet metal is one of the quickest and most efficient methods available for removing paint and rust, providing it is done delicately. In response to people who say sandblasting will blow a hole through weak metal, he says, "If the metal is so weak that you're going to blow a hole through it, it needs to be repaired anyway."

For anything but the heaviest gauge steel, make sure you or the commercial operator use fine silica sand, glass beads, or plastic. Keep plenty of distance between the nozzle and the steel to avoid warping or stretching the part. Always keep the nozzle moving. If the metal gets too hot, it will end up having ripples that are virtually impossible to remove.

Jim Deardorff, who has stripped hundreds of cars and tractors in his career, says he has developed his own way to media blast sheet metal. A few years ago, he developed Classic Blast, a special blasting

Opinions vary widely on media blasting sheet metal. While some restorers limit media blasting to cast parts such as wheels and engine blocks, others use fine silica sand to strip the paint on sheet metal, as well. If you use a sandblaster near engine parts, though, make sure every hole that could allow sand to enter the engine is plugged, including water-pump vents. Also remove electrical components such as the generator and starter.

If you have access to a cabinet-type sandblaster that uses glass beads, even small parts like the shell for a headlight can be sandblasted.

mix made up of aluminum oxide, ground black walnut shells, and his own blend of other materials, including some garnet. Using the product in a closed-top sandblast pot, which uses a vacuum to pull the media into the chamber, he says he can reduce the pressure to as little as 35 pounds and still clean fragile parts without damage. To prove it, he often demonstrates the effectiveness of his sandblast method by removing the paint from an aluminum pop can that's still filled with liquid.

Since the walnuts shells in the blend tend to polish the sheet metal as they assist in paint removal, Deardorff says the stripped surface is also less prone to rust than if other types of media are used. The

To demonstrate the gentle action of his Classic Blast material on sheet metal, Deardorff has been known to sandblast one-half of a soft drink can. His special blend is composed of aluminum oxide, ground black walnut shells, and his own blend of other materials, including garnet.

Jim Deardorff media blasts sheet metal by putting his own blend of Classic Blast material in a closed-top sandblast pot that uses a vacuum to pull the media into the chamber. That allows him to reduce the pressure to as little as 35 pounds and still clean fragile parts without damage. The key is using a large nozzle and holding it at an angle to strip away material quickly.

There's a definite difference between the silica sand used for media blasting and the Classic Blast mix (in left bucket), which uses ground walnut shells as a major component.

Deardorff routinely uses his media mixture to strip paint from a wide variety of sheetmetal panels for customers. The John Deere tractor hood and garden tractor hood shown here are just a few examples. However, he has also stripped classic automobile bodies and even a jet airplane.

While it's not as easy as using a sandblaster, using a wire brush on an electric grinder can take off years of accumulated rust, according to Estel Theis of Savannah, Missouri.

walnut shells also soften the impact of the more aggressive material in the mix.

Chemical Stripping

Another paint removal method that is widely practiced by a number of restorers, particularly to remove paint from sheetmetal parts, is using a quality metal stripper. Unlike media blasting, using chemical strippers doesn't pose any risk of warping or pitting the sheet metal. Still, it can remove multiple layers of paint, primer, wax, and rust rather easily. Another advantage of chemical paint strippers is that they can often be as effective as media blasting, yet they won't warp or affect the metal in any way.

Just keep in mind that chemical strippers are generally toxic and require adequate ventilation. In addition, you should always wear eye protection and rubber gloves when using them.

Your local automotive parts dealer should be able to direct you to a wide assortment of paint strippers for cleaning sheet metal down to bare metal. Many restorers say they have the best luck with aircraft paint remover (far right).

Safety First

Although sandblasting or media blasting, as it is more commonly called, is an effective way to remove old paint and rust, it does require a certain amount of caution and preparation. Depending upon the job and the air pressure behind it, media can be propelled at speeds up to 400 miles per hour, which means it can easily penetrate skin.

That's why it's important that you protect yourself while doing any type of sandblasting. That means wearing heavy-duty leather gloves, long sleeves, and a good-quality sandblasting hood.

It's also important that you wear a National Institute for Occupational Safety and Health (NIOSH)–approved respirator to protect yourself from media particles and paint debris, as well as dirt and rust particles that are dislodged and floating in the air.

You should be able to find all of these items from any business that sells sandblasting equipment and media, at your paint supplier, or from your local auto supply store.

Perhaps the best option for stripping sheet metal if you're doing the job yourself is using aircraft stripper. It may have been formulated at one time for aircraft sheet metal, but it's available at any paint and automotive supply store. For best results, it generally helps to scuff the old paint surface prior to any application. It doesn't matter whether you use coarse sandpaper or a rough pad, such as those marketed by Scotch-Brite. The idea is to scratch the surface enough to allow the paint stripper to penetrate deeper into the paint coating.

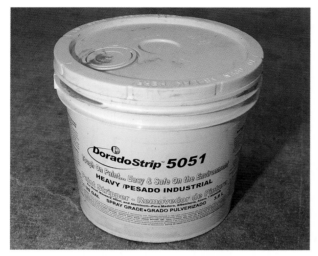

In addition to media blasting, Jim Deardorff also uses a chemical stripper at times. However, he prefers a product called DoradoStrip that claims to contain no toxic or hazardous air pollutants.

A number of parts, like the steering shaft, will require hand sanding, due to their shape. Any part that can bind or stick should be refinished to like-new condition.

As mentioned earlier, some restorers like to use a combination of processes, such as using a paint stripper followed by media blasting, particularly on components like the engine, transmission, and frame. Jim Deardorff is one of those restorers. Furthermore, he says he has found a water-based stripper called DoradoStrip that he likes better than any of the chemical-based strippers. Even though it contains no toxic or hazardous air pollutants, he says it effectively lifts epoxies, urethanes, and powder coatings.

Deardorff typically applies the material to any surface he wants to strip, then lets it soak overnight before washing it off the next morning with a strong stream of water. Most of the paint, he insists, washes right off with the material.

Paint Stripper Application

Before applying chemical strippers of any kind, it's important that you mask off any areas that you don't intend to strip, just as you would if you were going to media blast the area. In this case, it's best to apply a double layer of masking tape or other material. Be careful, too, to make sure you cover any crevices that could allow the material to seep into an area that you don't intend to strip. Any chemical residue that isn't removed will prevent paint from adhering to the area later on.

Ford collectors who have been fortunate enough to acquire a 1939 Model 9N with an aluminum hood leave the aluminum parts unpainted and polish them to a bright shine. Only around 700 tractors were built before the aluminum hood was replaced with steel, so it's only natural for a Ford enthusiast to show it off.

This is a good example of an engine hood that has been stripped and prepared. All that is left to do here is to prime and paint.

As for application, it's best to read and follow the directions on the container. Unless you're using a product that comes in an aerosol can or instructs you to apply it with a hand sprayer, it generally works best to use a cheap bristle-type brush and apply the stripper in one direction only. Don't be too conservative, either. If you get it too thin, you'll just end up repeating the process.

Next, allow time for the stripper to work into the paint layer before scraping it off with a putty knife, steel wool, or a special pad. In most cases, this is at least 15 minutes or until the paint has completely softened. If you start scraping the paint off too soon, you'll also remove the stripper before it has a chance to work deeper. Even then, it may be necessary to apply more stripper as undercoats are exposed.

Once you've stripped away all the loose paint and exposed the bare metal, it's important that you neutralize any stripper material that remains with plenty of clean water. If you haven't used them to this point, a fine steel wool or a fine-grade cleaning pad work well to remove any paint particles. These also will hold enough water to help dilute the stripper at the same time.

The final step, after all paint and stripper residue has been removed, is to dry the surface and wipe it down with a quality wax and grease remover. If the surface isn't going to be coated with a filler primer or another type of primer for immediate painting, you should also finish it off with a coat of epoxy primer to prevent any rust from forming on the bare surface.

If you can find someone to do it for you, another good way to strip paint from sheetmetal parts is to dip them in a caustic soda bath. A lye solution is added so that any grease that may be on a part is removed. You may need to check around with some of the automotive repair shops or tractor or auto restorers to find someone in your area that specializes in this type of service. Don't try to do it yourself, though, even if you find a lye-based paint remover recipe on the internet. Lye can burn skin and clothing just as quickly and easily as acid. It just happens to be on the other end of the pH spectrum.

If you do take the parts to a professional paint stripper, it's still important that you rinse and dry each of the parts once you get them back and then coat them with an epoxy primer as soon as possible.

CHAPTER 5

SHEETMETAL REPAIR

Once you have all the paint off, the first thing you're going to notice on an older tractor are all the dents, dings, scratches, and rust spots that need to be filled in, pounded out, and otherwise hidden from view. You may even have to splice in one or two pieces of sheet metal, create a new bracket, or, in the worst-case scenario, fabricate a whole new sheetmetal section. This is particularly true if you're trying to restore a vintage tractor that hasn't been used for a half century.

Rust Repair

Depending on the age of the tractor you're painting and how long it has been sitting around in the weather, rust is often a bigger problem with sheet metal than dents and dings. That's particularly true of an older tractor you intend to restore. Unless you're lucky enough to find one that has spent the last 50 years in a barn, chances are it was parked out in a tree row or pasture once the owner thought its life was over.

The first thing you need to do is determine the extent of the rust damage. Is it just surface rust, or does it go deeper? If the rust has gone all the way through

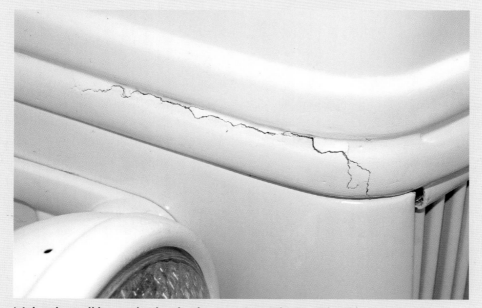

It's hard to tell here whether body putty is cracking under the paint or rust is working its way through from the backside. What appears to have been a nice paint job, though, is going to waste.

the sheet metal, you'll need to consider two options. One is to replace the entire piece, as mentioned in the previous chapter. That's easy enough to do if you're looking at a hood or fender for a vintage John Deere B, a Farmall M, or a Ford 8N. But that isn't an option with some of the less-popular brands, or with a rare model like an orchard version. In those situations, you'll have to cut out and repair the hole with a patch as covered later in this chapter.

If the rust is only on the surface and there is solid metal behind it, you can often sand it out with 80- to 100-grit sandpaper, wipe the entire surface down with a wax and grease remover, and apply a coat of epoxy primer to protect against any additional rust.

If the rust goes a little deeper or includes pitting, another option is to carefully sandblast the surface as described in the previous chapter. That will still leave a lot of deep pits, though, which will need to be filled with one or more applications of filler primer or, perhaps, a light coat of body putty.

Dents and Creases

While it's unfortunate, it's not unusual to find one or more dents and/or creases in a tractor's sheet metal. Being the work tool that it was or still is, dents just seem to happen, particularly if the tractor is equipped with a front-end loader. The fenders seem to be a vulnerable area on most tractors, too, as they often come in contact with everything from

You can add as many coats of paint as you want, and you still won't hide the dents and wrinkles in the sheet metal on this tractor. In fact, a coat of paint just makes them show up even more. It would have been better to replace the panel or spend some time on bodywork before getting to this point.

If you have many dents to remove, you may want to invest in a bodyman's hammer and dolly.

Small dents in sheet metal can often be removed with a ball-peen hammer and a mallet or a large hammer to back up the piece. On stubborn dents, however, it may be necessary to apply heat to help shrink the metal back into place.

From a distance, this tractor looks like a quality restoration . . . until you get close enough to notice the dent in the fuel tank.

tree limbs and fence posts to towed implements on a tight turn.

If a dent or crease is more than 1/8 inch deep, it's best to smooth it out with a body repairman's hammer and dolly. Do not simply fill it in with body putty. Not only is the area likely to crack or sag if it is too deep, but the vibration that is inherent with tractor operation can cause body putty to pop right out of a deep dent, leaving you with an ugly hole that will require more work and a new coat of paint.

If there aren't a lot of dents to take care of, you might be able to fix them with a ball-peen hammer and a mallet or large hammer to back up the piece. The thing you have to keep in mind is that the original metal stretched as the dent was created. So you may have to shrink it as it is straightened. One way to do that is to heat the spot with an oxygen-acetylene torch before beating out the dent.

Another technique, particularly if you are trying to remove a sharp crease, is to drill or punch a series of small holes (approximately 1/16 inch in diameter) along the crease. This will allow the metal to shift as it goes back into place. The holes can be filled later with epoxy or filler putty. If you're drilling holes in the panel, this also gives you the opportunity to use a dent puller instead of a hammer and dolly (although you may need them to finish the job).

When straightening any type of dent or crease, it's important that you don't go too far and end up with an outward bulge. If that ends up being the case, you'll need to carefully hammer the high spot back into the contour. In essence, the repaired area needs to be slightly lower than the surrounding area so the body filler can be matched to the undamaged surface. But that isn't possible if the dent ends up being higher than the surrounding surface.

Repairing Holes and Installing Patches

If the damage you're trying to repair is too severe, you may just want to replace the entire component, such as the hood, side panel, or fender. For newer tractors and any of the popular restoration models, these are readily available.

A number of materials on the market, including brands such as Liquid Steel and J-B Weld, can be used to repair metal parts that shouldn't be subjected to a lot of pressure.

The engine side panels found on many Oliver and Cockshutt tractors were some of the first parts to disappear and are currently some of the hardest to locate.

There may be some instances, however, that call for cutting out an old piece of metal and welding in a new piece. If you decide to do this, first remove all the paint from the area to be worked, if you haven't already done so. At least two inches of solid, bare metal should surround the area to be replaced. Next, make a clean cut around the damaged area so you have removed all the bad metal and have left a clean, solid edge.

Although tin snips might work in some situations, the best way to cut out the area is to use a die grinder with a cut-off wheel, a plasma cutter, or a reciprocating saw. It's important that you cut beyond the damage because when you take the pieces to a welder, or do the work yourself, any thin, pitted surfaces will self-destruct. You'll also want to remove the section in a shape that will be easy to reproduce. A square section with clean right angles tends to work best.

Now, find a scrap piece of sheet metal that is the same thickness or gauge as the original piece. The biggest mistake people make at this stage is to use a slightly thicker or thinner replacement piece. Next, you'll want to trace the hole you have created onto a piece of cardboard and make yourself a template. This will be particularly helpful when you go to cut out the new piece.

If necessary, bend the new piece to match the contour of the hood, grille, or fender where it is being

One option to consider instead of getting new replacement parts is to search out original salvaged parts that need a little work. One place to find these is in the vendor section at many tractor shows.

Even replacement dash panels and replacement nose pieces are available from a number of sources if your old piece is unusable.

There may be times when it is necessary to splice in a new piece of metal to replace a rusted-out area. The answer is to spot-weld a metal piece of comparable thickness in place and then cover the patch with body filler. The entire area can then be sanded to a thin layer that only covers imperfections.

installed. Finally, clamp or tape the new piece into position and tack weld it in place being careful not to set the welder at a temperature that is too high and would cause it to burn through the sheet metal.

To make it easier to hold the patch in place, you may want to follow the lead of some body shops and use a body hammer to form a depression for the patch material. Simply tap the hammer around the outside of the opening until the surrounding good metal has formed a depression that is about one inch wider on each side than the dimensions of the hole. It should also be just deep enough to allow the patch to rest flush with or just slightly below the surrounding metal. Naturally, the patch will need to be a little larger so it overlaps the good metal by a half to three-fourths of an inch in each direction. This method also gives you the option of using

rivets or screws instead of welds—as long as they can be ground down far enough and covered with body filler when you complete the repair.

As you finish welding around the splice, you also need to be careful not to heat the area to the point where it warps or disfigures the sheet metal. It generally works best to skip around or alternate between the different sides of the patch to avoid building up too much heat in one spot. Another trick some bodywork specialists use is to grab the air hose from your compressor and blow cool air onto the welds as you move around the patch.

In the process, try to hide as much of the weld as possible. If you use a series of spot welds around the patch, you can fill in the seam with body putty a little later. Finally, to complete the patch, grind the welds down to remove any high spots, and fill the area with J-B Weld, body filler, or Bondo (see the Using Body Filler section, which follows). This will also fill any rust pits and gaps that have been left. Once the filler has hardened, you can sand it down to the point where the patch is flush with the clean sheet metal, using finer and finer sandpaper to finish the surface.

If you recall from Chapter 2, one likely spot for repair on early-model John Deere two-cylinder tractors is around the exhaust pipe where it exits through the hood. As mentioned earlier, a lot of original owners didn't go through the effort to remove the hood, steering shaft, and grille just to replace a muffler. So they simply cut or peeled away enough of the hood to reach the bolts from the top.

The good news is that there is now a patch available to correct the problem on Model A and B tractors. Available through Moline Tractor and Plow Company, among other sources, the patch is already sized and contoured to fit the back side of the hood. Plus, it has a raised section that surrounds the exhaust pipe hole that is the exact thickness of the hood. As a result, all you have to do is cut a clean, square hole large enough to accept the raised lip and carefully weld the patch to the underside of the hood as previously explained. Then, simply fill the gap between the hood and the patch and sand it smooth.

If you're dealing with rather small holes in a sheetmetal component, you can often get by with putting a piece of fiberglass cloth on the back side of the cavity and filling it with Bondo or body filler. It may take several thin coats before you get the hole filled to surface level. At that point, you can sand and treat it just as you would any other patch. For fiberglass patches, it's best to purchase a complete fiberglass repair kit, which includes nearly everything you'll need for the job, including the fiberglass cloth, liquid or jelly epoxy, release film, and hardener. The kit will also contain the

There may come a time when you actually have to fabricate a part or hire a metal worker to do it for you. After a fruitless search for a new grille for a vintage Cletrac crawler, Bill Anderson, a full-time tractor restorer from Superior, Nebraska, simply built one himself.

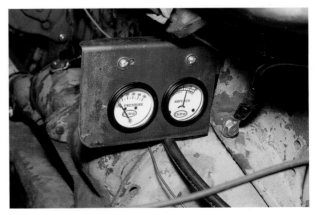

A new gauge panel was among the other items fabricated by Anderson while he was rebuilding the Cletrac.

John Deere owners were notorious for peeling back the hood around the exhaust to save time during a muffler replacement. That's because you had to remove the hood, steering shaft, and everything connected to get to the bolts. Cutting a hole around the bolts was a lot faster.

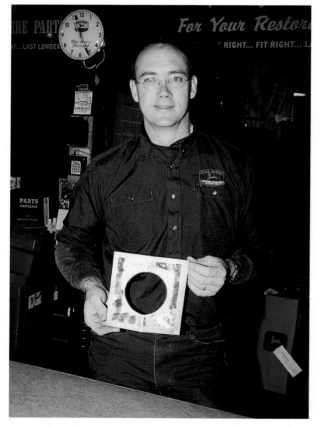

A number of sources, including the Moline Tractor and Plow Company, offer patches to repair the hood area surrounding the exhaust on A or B model tractors.

Because of its somewhat fragile nature, the corrugated screen used in many tractor grilles is often torn, dented, or gouged. Fortunately, replacement material is available.

A new grille screen makes a tremendous difference in the appearance of this restoration.

Don't be surprised if large sheetmetal parts like fenders and hoods don't fit perfectly when it comes time to reassemble the tractor—particularly if you had to apply heat to a part. It doesn't take much to shift a bolt hole ever so slightly.

appropriate instructions for installing a patch on sheetmetal damage.

Using Body Filler

Unless you're simply repainting a tractor that's already been restored, or you're not bothered by a few dents on a work tractor, chances are you're going to need to use some plastic body filler or Bondo.

The first thing that's necessary, if you haven't already done so as part of the rust removal or repair process, is to sand the area down to bare metal. The process of sanding away the paint should also reveal any other high or low spots in the area. Now switch to a 100-grit sanding disc and feather any remaining paint out to at least an inch from the dented area. Finally, clean the repair area with wax/silicone remover to get it as clean as possible.

Now that you're ready for the plastic filler, mix the appropriate amount of filler with the hardener. If you don't have a mixing palate, you can easily substitute a clean piece of cardboard. Just be sure you get the two components mixed thoroughly. If there are streaks in the filler, you haven't folded and stirred it enough yet. It should all be one color when properly mixed.

Once the hardener has been added, the material will begin to stiffen rather quickly, so don't mix

With the paint removed from this hood piece, it's ready to be finished off with a little body filler for a glass-smooth surface.

For the extra strength needed on some patches, you might want to consider something other than plastic body filler, such as this metal-reinforced filler.

Your local auto parts supplier can direct you to everything you'll need to fill and cover minor imperfections. Just remember that body filler or Bondo should not be used to correct deep dents or creases.

When mixing body filler, it's important to get the right mix of material and hardener. Otherwise, the material may begin to harden before you have a chance to spread an even coat.

Just as when you were removing rust and old paint, you may need to do some hand sanding and use some elbow grease when doing bodywork on your tractor.

Depending on the brand, some body fillers allow you to start shaping the material with a cheese grater–type file before the material has hardened. Others recommend No. 30 grit sandpaper for initial shaping.

more than you can spread in a few minutes. Using too much hardener will only speed the hardening process, so be careful about overdoing it.

Now, using a body filler spreader, work the filler into the dented or damaged area using long, smooth strokes, or use the spreader to apply a thin film over the rust-pitted section. Be sure you apply a reasonable amount of pressure during application to ensure good adhesion with the surface. In the meantime, always follow the directions on the particular brand you are using, as it may differ on application instructions. As soon as the filler starts to ball up under the spreader, it's generally time to stop and mix up a new batch. Don't worry about getting filler on the unsanded area or any remaining paint. You'll be sanding off the excess and feathering it out as soon as it cures.

Generally, you can start shaping the area as soon as the filler has dried to where you can still scratch it with your fingernail. In other words, it shouldn't

Once any added body filler has hardened, it should be sanded to a smooth finish that is flush with the original sheetmetal surface, using finer and finer grit paper as you finish it off.

Estel Theis uses a straight-edge ruler to check for any remaining depressions while using body filler on a nose piece.

be completely hardened. At this point, you can begin rough shaping the material with a Surform or cheese-grater file.

On the other hand, some plastic fillers recommend the material be completely hardened before you start working it or that it can be worked with an 80-grit sanding disc mounted on an electric drill. So be sure you read the instructions for the material you're using.

Don't worry if you end up with a low spot or a place where a bubble has formed. All you have to do is mix up a little more filler and apply another light layer. In fact, it's better to build up the filler in several layers on large or deep areas, rather than trying to apply one thick coat. There's less chance

of forming bubbles or leaving voids this way, and you'll end up with a smoother patch. Just remember to decrease the angle of the applicator with each ensuing layer.

Here are a couple of other tips: If you're applying filler to a large flat area, start with a light strip of filler near one edge and then overlap the next few strips by about a third until you get to the opposite edge. This automatically places the heaviest amount of filler near the center of the repair. Also, if you're applying filler to a curved surface, use an applicator made from soft plastic or hard rubber so the filler can be shaped to the contour of the surface.

Once the entire area has hardened and you're satisfied with the patch contour, you can begin final shaping with coarse 80- to 100-grit sandpaper. Don't forget to wear an approved dust-filtering mask!

Whether you use a Surform file or course-grit sandpaper for the initial shaping, make sure you leave enough material to allow for finish sanding, which will allow you to sand out all the rough file marks and course sanding scratches.

Move the sander back and forth, up and down, and diagonally over the entire area, switching to finer grades of sandpaper until it blends in with the surrounding surface. After every two or three minutes of sanding, run your hand over the surface to determine the progress. Any irregularities will show up clearly when covered with paint, so it's best to find them now. Also, check the area where it blends into the surrounding sheet metal for any rough spots. No matter the pattern, try to blend as much multidirectional movement as possible into the job to prevent grooves and potential patterns. Regardless of where the filler is used, the key to a smooth, flat surface is a long sanding board or DA sander for finish work. While a short sanding block follows the contours, a long board tends to bridge the high spots, so they can be worked down to a level surface. Finish up with 180 grit or finer sandpaper until the filler material has been perfectly smoothed and feathered into the surrounding area.

Ed Hoyt of St. Joseph, Missouri, smoothes out a spot on the fender of a Model D he recently restored.

Fortunately, the hood on this 520 didn't need much filler or bodywork to get it ready for painting.

Using long sanding boards, whether you're sanding by hand or with a power sander, will help ensure a smooth surface when finishing body filler or a coat of primer.

CHAPTER 6
PREPARATION FOR PAINTING

Even though you've spent the last few chapters—and who knows how many hours—stripping paint and making sheetmetal repairs, you're still not quite ready to start painting. The good news, though, is that you're getting close.

Unless you totally media blasted every inch of the tractor, chances are some areas are still covered with old paint. And applying any primer and new paint without scuffing up the old surface would be a mistake. Paint must have an absorbent base to adhere to. If you removed the old paint to bare metal, or if the paint that is left is tight with no chance of flaking off later, then using a fine grade of Scotch-Brite pads works well for scuffing the surface, particularly on hard paint surfaces. Just be sure the old paint feathers into the bare metal surfaces without any hard edges. A coat of filler primer will generally take care of any differences later.

The one advantage of painting a tractor, in comparison to an automobile, is that the surface is usually rougher to begin with, which gives the paint something to hold on to. That is especially true of the cast components, like the engine, frame, and transmission. It's the sheet metal that will be of greater concern.

Once all surfaces have been stripped, cleaned, and smoothed or filled, it's time to make sure the tractor and the sheetmetal panels have been thoroughly cleaned of any stripping residue or media blasting material.

Make Sure It's Clean

Perhaps the most obvious advice for preparing the tractor for painting is to make sure it is clean. If you previously media blasted the tractor to remove paint, make sure you have gone over the entire unit with an air hose to remove any medium from cracks and joints. Similarly, if you used a chemical stripper, make sure every trace of the product has been removed and neutralized with clean water. Finally, make sure that you've removed the dust and residue from any body filler you've used and that you have wiped all sheetmetal surfaces with a tack cloth to remove dust and debris that may have settled. That applies, too, to any dust created by scuffing old paint. In fact, if at all possible, you should go over the whole tractor with soap and water, just to make sure you've got everything.

At this point, some automotive paint books will tell you to use a wax/silicone remover solvent on all surfaces that will be painted. Again, that's because paints need a rough, but clean surface for adhesion. However, most automotive painters are now using urethane, while most tractor painters are still using enamel. Not only is the latter more forgiving, but you're dealing with a lot of cast-iron and heavy-gauge sheet metal as opposed to glass-smooth engine hoods and fiberglass fender panels. Perhaps the best bet is to talk to your paint supplier to see if he or she recommends any additional cleaner.

Jim Deardorff, owner of Superior Coatings in Chillicothe, Missouri, says he has had good luck with a product he recently discovered called Picklex 20. Although he hasn't had many months to test it long-term, he notes that it can be applied to any metal surface as a combination metal surface cleaner, surface rust remover, surface preparation, and pre-treatment for finishing. The product also promises to provide long-term rust protection on surfaces that have been prepped, but are waiting on a sealer or primer coat, to prevent oxidation.

Deardorff says he has also used a product called Chlor*Wash to clean tractors prior to painting. Because it was initially developed for industrial use, Chlor*Wash is actually blended to remove road films, dirt, and chloride, as well as sulfate and nitrate

Jim Deardorff often uses a product called Chlor*Wash to clean surfaces a final time before they're painted to remove salt, dirt, and exhaust residue. He often uses the same product to wash restored tractors after they've been exposed to the elements.

salts. In essence, it has the cleaning ability of a soap but has the added feature of removing any salts.

Masking

To protect components or parts from primer and paint, they need to be covered with masking paper and/or tape. Perhaps you've done this to some extent already, if you did any media blasting. Masking for media blasting and masking for paint, however, are really two different things.

One way to mask a large opening is to cut a piece of cardboard to cover the void and punch holes for any bolt holes.

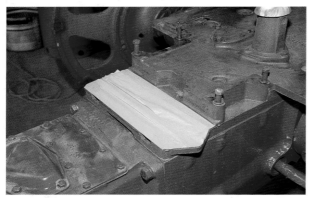

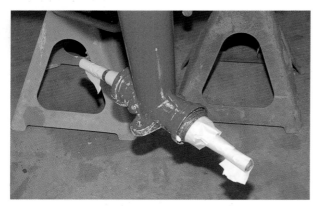

Make sure all openings have been covered and any parts you don't want painted have been masked. That includes wheel spindles, the distributor, gauges, etc.

As you learned earlier, the purpose of masking prior to media blasting is to protect vulnerable areas from the effects of sandblasting or media blasting and to keep sand and material from getting into areas where it can cause damage. These areas include brake adjustment holes, water pump drain holes, and open bolt holes. That generally requires something more substantial than a single layer of paper or tape.

The purpose of paint masking is to prevent unwanted paint from covering an area. Fortunately, you shouldn't need to do a lot of masking on a tractor. Most of the parts that need to be protected from paint can simply be removed, including the glass fuel sediment bowl, the muffler, and tires. That also applies to emblems and nameplates. It is far easier to remove these types of parts than to try to mask them, and it will take less time in the long run, too.

The other advantage you'll have with most tractors is that most, if not all, of the tractor will be painted the same color. Even if the sheet metal happens to be a different color, it will have been removed so you can paint the frame and engine separately. That really just leaves items such as the headlight lenses; mating surfaces, which require a gasket; wheel spindles; and/or wheel hubs that will need to be masked.

You certainly don't want to paint something as unique as the brass carburetor or vintage magneto on some early tractor models. Either mask them carefully, or remove them altogether and carefully mask the engine openings.

The one exception will be those tractor models that have a two-tone hood or grille. Examples include Oliver tractors on which the grille is painted red with a yellow center stripe; the Ford Powermaster line, which has a red band down the center of the gray hood; and John Deere's 30 Series two-cylinder models like the 530 and 630, which have a green hood with a yellow stripe down the side. In each of these cases, you'll need to prime the entire piece, but mask off the individual areas for painting.

One of the most important things about masking is to make sure you have quality tape and that it is relatively fresh. If tape gets too old and brittle, it can be extremely hard to work with and even harder

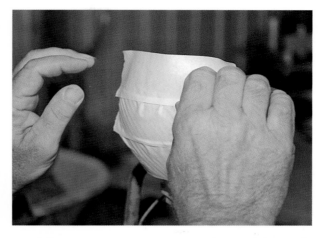

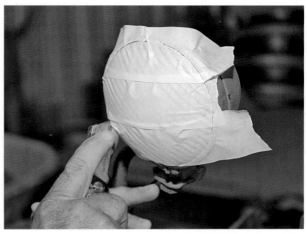

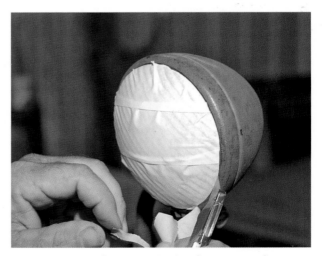

One way to mask an area is simply to cover the entire surface and then cut away the excess with a sharp knife.

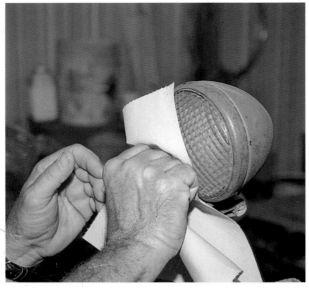

If necessary, clean the surface you'll be masking to make sure the tape doesn't come loose or lift at an edge while you're applying paint.

to remove. That's one advantage of the new blue plastic painter's tape that came out a few years ago. It provides more time to finish the job and remove the tape than the average roll of masking tape. The bottom line is that an automotive paint store is probably a better source for materials than the local discount store.

Speaking of materials, the same logic goes for masking paper. Granted, you may be tempted to use newspaper, and that may be fine for masking some parts. But it's not your best option when masking something that really needs to be protected. Newspaper tends to tear much more easily than masking paper designed for the job. Paint can also seep through if the newspaper becomes too saturated, particularly if the paint has been thinned quite a bit to work in your spray gun. Lastly, newspaper doesn't lie as flat on most surfaces as masking paper does. That leaves pockets that can pick up

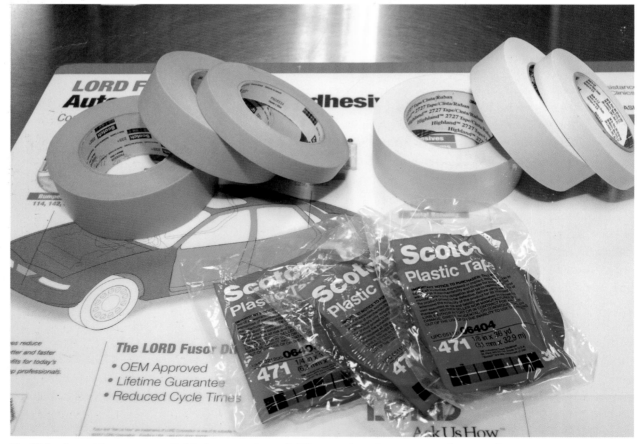

You'll find masking tape available in a number of different sizes from your paint supplier.

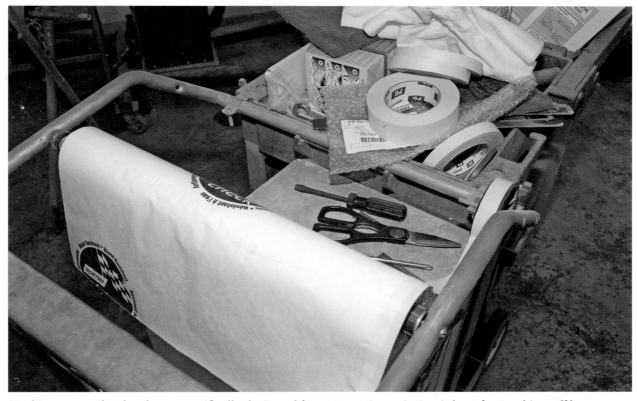

Masking paper that has been specifically designed for automotive painting is best for masking off large areas, such as the two-toned hood on some tractor models.

dust and dirt that has been kicked up while you're making other preparations. The next thing you know, that dust and dirt have been transferred and are now embedded in the paint surface.

If you're masking off an area of the hood that is to be a different color, you may want to start with a narrow roll of tape that is only 1/8- to 1/4-inch wide. This is particularly important if you have to deal with any curves, as it's much easier to follow the contours with the narrow width. Then you can come back with a wider piece of tape and your paper to completely cover the unpainted portion.

Also, if you're painting a two-tone tractor, like a Farmall 350 or 450, that has white panels on the red hood or a John Deere 530 or 630 that has the yellow panel on the side of a predominantly green hood, most restorers suggest masking the hood and painting the smaller areas first. Then go back and carefully mask off the entire white or yellow panel while you paint the remainder of the hood. This is

If you use newspaper for masking, make sure it is smooth and doesn't contain pockets that can gather and hold dust. Also, make sure you use enough layers to keep paint from seeping through to the surface below.

Unless you're painting a newer tractor or a classic model like the Minneapolis-Moline UDLX, which featured a cab as early as 1938, you probably won't need to worry about masking off any glass surfaces. If you do, however, simply use wide masking tape and masking paper to cover both the rubber molding and the glass.

a little easier on most two-tone Ford tractor hoods because the colors, in most cases, are separated by a seam or panel edge.

When laying down masking tape, it's generally best to use the longest strips possible. Every seam you make leaves the potential for a leak. On the other hand, you don't want to start weaving in an attempt to lay one strip over too much distance. If you prefer to use shorter strips that overlap and you've done a good job of sticking them down, then do it your own way. If you're working on a vertical surface, though, and you're putting on more than one strip, start from the bottom and go up, so the upper strips overlap the lower ones.

No matter what your technique is, lay the tape down evenly without stretching it. Then cut it off cleanly with a trim knife, razor blade, or X-Acto knife, rather than tearing it. Tearing it just leaves more ragged edges that can allow paint to seep under the tape.

Finally, if you're painting a tractor with a cab, you'll need to mask around the edge molding first. The best way to do this is to run a 1- or 1½-inch-wide strip of masking tape over the molding around the window. Then come back with masking paper to cover the glass. Attach the masking paper to the first strip of tape with more tape, making sure you've covered all the seams between the two.

Masking Tires

As mentioned earlier, it's always easiest to remove the tires before painting the wheels. If you're painting a restoration tractor, you've probably done this anyway so you can check the condition of the wheel rim for rust. Or you may have needed to replace one or more tires that were badly rotted or weather checked. If that was the case, you can simply sandblast the wheels and prepare them for painting as you would any other part; otherwise, you'll need to mask the rubber.

If any part of the tractor has to remain outdoors, it is a good idea to protect it with a coat of primer as soon as it has been cleaned and prepped.

With most tractor brands and models, the wheels are a different color than the rest of the tractor or the frame. That's not the case with a Model 9N or 2N Ford, as the entire tractor is painted the same color. But it's true on most everything else.

Consequently, you'll need to cover any wheels and/or tires that haven't been removed until you've painted the rest of the frame, engine, and other components that have a different color. One way to do this is by covering smaller wheels with plastic trash bags. In the same manner, you can use larger sheets of plastic or plastic drop cloths to cover the rear tires and wheels. Use tape where necessary to hold them in place, and be careful about letting dust accumulate in any folds.

Once you finish the main part of the tractor, you'll need to mask off the rubber tires with tape and masking paper and paint them separately. You'll also need to protect the rest of the tractor from overspray if the wheels haven't been removed. Considering that you'll need to mask and paint both sides of each wheel, you can see why it's in your best interest to put the tractor on stands and remove the wheels at the start of the job. The same goes for the tires.

Granted, not everyone has the means to haul a set of tractor tires to the local tire shop, but most farm cooperatives have a mobile tire service that supports farmers with field repairs. So it may just be worth your time and effort to have them make two stops at your shop, too: once to remove the tires from the wheels and once more to put them back on when the paint has cured.

CHAPTER 7

THE PRIMER COAT

Once the sheet metal has been stripped, smoothed, and filled as necessary and the body and frame have been cleaned and prepared, it's time to apply a quality coat of primer. Some restorers recommend applying a coat of etch primer immediately after the tractor frame and/or sheet metal have been cleaned, even if they won't be painted for a while. According to Gary Ledford, a paint technician from St. Joseph, Missouri, bare metal can begin to rust in as little as four hours. Consequently, a coat of etch primer on bare metal not only helps

You'll find several different kinds of primers on the market, including filler primers and those that are self-etching, as well as epoxy and urethane primers. Your paint supplier can help you select the best type for your needs and application.

Dave Henderson, a tractor repair and restoration specialist from Colo, Iowa, applies a coat of primer to a vintage Farmall tractor.

In most cases, the primer is applied in the same manner as paint. Consequently, it's important to follow the same procedures you'll find in Chapter 10.

prevent rust, but may make it easier to clean away any grease or oil before you add additional primer coats or the paint coat.

The primer stage also gives you the opportunity to take care of a lot of the imperfections that may remain after most of the bodywork has been completed. By putting on two or three coats of filler primer, you can easily fill a lot of pits and crevices.

Choosing the Right Primer Type

A number of different types of primers can be used to prepare, fill, or seal the surface prior to the final coat of paint. Each has its own unique role and application. For example, while epoxy and urethane primers protect components from new rust, some form a harder finish than others. However, you need to ensure that the primer you select is not only compatible with any paint that remains on the tractor or engine, but also with the paint you have selected to finish the project.

Ledford explains that the type of primer you start with depends to some extent on the type of finish you're covering—old paint, bare metal, or cast iron. If an alkyd enamel is being applied over lacquer, which is often the case with classic tractors if they haven't been totally stripped or media blasted, a sealer *must* be used. A sealer should also be used with enamel over enamel. Basically, the bottom line is that if you're in doubt about the old paint or primer, use a sealer.

Epoxy Primers

If you're shooting primer over bare metal or cast iron that could be exposed to the weather before you get it covered with additional primer, Ledford generally recommends using epoxy or self-etch-type primer. This is particularly the case with parts of the frame or cast wheels that have been sandblasted and are in no need of further work or sanding.

Epoxy is generally the easiest to use because, in many cases, depending on the brand, it combines the qualities of a metal etch, a primer surfacer, and a primer sealer in one product. A self-etching primer, on the other hand, is basically a phosphoric-acid-type etch. Self-etching primers have to have another primer over the top of them, Ledford adds. It can't be an epoxy primer, but it can be a urethane primer. Ledford cautions, however, that you need to check with your paint supplier to learn the characteristics of each product, as these principles don't apply to all brands.

You normally cannot paint directly onto a self-etching primer because the paint won't adhere. That's why painters generally recommend that tractor restorers go over bare finishes with an epoxy primer, since it will give you a more durable finish, and it will etch aluminum and metal in one shot.

Although epoxy primer is primarily used for corrosion protection, it can be used in two other ways. It can be used as a primer-sealer, where you spray it on, wait 15 to 20 minutes, and start top coating with

Estel Theis shoots a coat of primer on the hood of a John Deere two-cylinder tractor. Note that primers tend to come in a variety of colors, depending on the type and manufacturer.

your color. Or it can be used as a primer-surfacer to cover minor flaws in the surface. In this case, you will want to put down two to three coats, giving it 15 to 20 minutes to dry between coats. Then, wait at least six hours before sanding the surface.

Finally, epoxy primer can be sprayed over the top of old lacquer paint—which was often used on older tractors—without a problem. It is a good idea, however, to seal the original lacquer just to be sure the two surfaces remain compatible. It is not recommended that you ever put lacquer on top of enamel.

"We have one epoxy primer in our inventory that can go right over a partially painted surface or bare metal," Ledford says. "Then, you can either paint over it when it dries or wait a few days to apply a top coat. The best part is it gives you a seven-day window to finish the job before it becomes necessary to resand it."

Urethane Primers

Although urethane primers are very popular with restorers due to their hard finish, they do not include any kind of chemical agent to prevent rusting. In fact, if you put a urethane filler primer over bare metal, it actually soaks up the moisture and the metal will begin to rust beneath the paint. Therefore, you either need to ensure that the surface is completely free of rust before you apply a urethane primer, or you need to lay down a coat of epoxy primer or an etching primer and put the urethane over it. Otherwise, you may find rust popping through the surface four or five months down the road.

Since urethane is only a primer-surfacer, you may need to apply a sealer of some kind before you paint, depending on the brand. Some let you paint right over the top as long as you haven't sanded through the primer layer. If not, a coat of epoxy primer over

Since the primer on this John Deere radiator is a dull yellow, it will make it easier to judge adequate paint coverage when it is ultimately painted green.

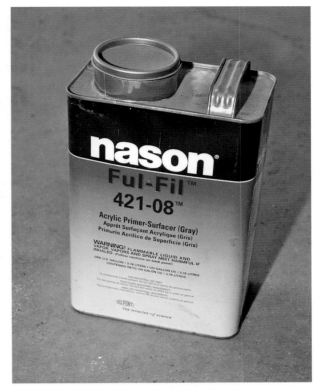

Filler primers have been described by some as "little more than liquid body filler," since they're formulated to fill and smooth surface imperfections.

the top will serve the purpose. Plus, a coat of epoxy will serve to bridge any scratches in the urethane that have been left after sanding and leave a smooth surface for the top-coat color.

The only thing you shouldn't do with urethane is put it under a top color coat of lacquer; however, since lacquer seems to be on its way out, the use of lacquer as a top coat isn't even covered in this book.

Lacquer Primers

Just like lacquer paint, lacquer primers are pretty much outdated. Although lacquer primers air dry fairly quickly, they tend to shrink for days and weeks after they have been applied. As a result, the primer can shrink for up to a month under any coat of paint that has been applied too early.

"If you use lacquer primer, it's best to let it set for at least a week minimum before you even do anything with it," paint technician Gary Ledford says. "And that's under perfect drying conditions . . . say 70 degrees or above; otherwise, you can start to see sanding scratches show up where it pulled away under the paint."

If you do use a lacquer primer, Ledford recommends putting a urethane-type primer over it before moving on to a top coat.

Filler Primers

For complete coverage of any imperfections, you might want to follow the lead of several tractor restorers and use a filler primer, heavy-bodied primer, or high-build primer on top of the etch primer or epoxy primer. No matter what you call it, a filler primer is basically formulated to fill in any pits in the surface from sanding or rust even quicker than an epoxy primer alone. As one restorer put it, filler primer is little more than a liquid body filler.

Although some tractor enthusiasts use fine-grit sandpaper, such as a No. 240 grit, to smooth the surface between coats of primer, others say they simply apply one coat of primer over the next, once it's had time to dry. On the last sanding before painting, though, you'll want to use an even finer sandpaper

When possible, go ahead and shoot a coat of primer on cast parts, like these wheel spindles, as soon as they have been stripped and prepped to prevent the formation of rust. They can wait a while for paint.

The same holds true for the tractor frame, which is generally constructed of cast iron.

sheet, like No. 400 grit, if you're using enamel, and up to No. 600 grit for urethane. At the very least, you will have to sand the surface before applying a sealer and the top coat. Because it has the texture to fill pits and imperfections in the sheet metal, an unsanded primer coat would be too rough to paint over without further preparation.

It's important to note, too, that most urethane primers will need a sealer coat before the top coat of color is applied, particularly if there is a chance you've sanded through in spots. In general, you can apply one coat of primer every 7 to 10 minutes, or when the first coat is dry to the touch. After the last coat, wait about three hours before sanding.

Jeff McManus, a John Deere enthusiast and former manager of the Moline Tractor and Plow Company, has been known to apply up to 15 coats of filler primer on a sheetmetal part that has had a lot of work done to it, just to get a glass-smooth surface. Between every three coats, he uses long sanding boards to smooth the finish. This helps prevent high and low spots from being formed by the sander itself.

Jeff Gravert, a Cockshutt enthusiast and professional restorer from Clay Center, Nebraska, says he has put as many as 20 coats of primer on a tractor, sanding between each coat. Regardless of how many coats he applies, though, he usually ends the sanding job with 600-grit sandpaper.

Another trick used by some body specialists is to switch between different colors of compatible primers so they can better identify hills and valleys in the finish. Be sure to finish with finer and finer grades of sandpaper, ultimately ending up with wet sanding paper.

Urethane primers are usually 1 to 3 millimeters thick per pass, Ledford explains, noting that one of his brands averages 2.5 millimeters per pass. So if you go around the tractor three times, you've got 7.5 millimeters of primer on there; whereas most new cars today have about 4.5 millimeters total, including all primers and paints. In the end, you'll have a much thicker paint coat.

Sealing Primers

The final step before applying a coat of paint should involve applying a coat of sealing primer, or sealer, as it's more commonly called. This closes the surface and prepares it to accept a coat of paint. The sealer does this in two ways. First, it helps minimize sand scratch swelling, which can make scratches more visible under the top coat. This is particularly important if you used a filler primer. If the sand marks aren't sealed, the paint solvent can cause the sand scratches to swell; plus, as solvents evaporate, paint solids fill the voids in the surface, leaving a microscopic series of hills and valleys, which results in a dull finish. In contrast, a coat of sealer provides a uniform base that, in turn, leads to uniform paint distribution and solvent evaporation.

Second, the sealer also acts as a barrier to protect the undercoat primers from any reaction with the top coat. Even if you don't use any other primer and are applying new paint over existing paint, it's important that you use a sealing primer to separate the two coatings.

As has been mentioned more than once in this book, enamel and urethane paints are totally incompatible with any lacquer-based paint or primer. If there's any doubt about what kind of primer to use at any stage of the painting process, it's best to discuss it with your paint supplier or refer to the applications guides and/or information sheets that are available for the products you plan to use. Regardless of what type of primer you use—and you'll probably need to use more than one type—you'll also need to mix it with thinner or reducer for it to be sprayable through a paint gun. Of course, your paint dealer can help with this decision, as well.

Before you apply any primer or sealer, though, use a tack cloth a second time to get the surface extra clean. You don't want to seal in any dirt or sanding dust.

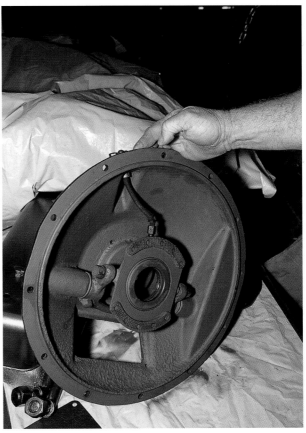

Covering tractor parts that have already been primed with a sheet of plastic will help prevent an accumulation of dust until it's time to paint.

Everything that will receive a coat of paint needs some kind of primer to seal the surface, including the fuel tank.

CHAPTER 8

SELECTING THE RIGHT PAINT TYPE

One of the most inexpensive options for tractor painting is implement enamel paint, which is generally available through farm supply stores and parts suppliers.

Most of the branded paint sold through the farm equipment dealers could also be classified as implement paint or synthetic enamel. Still, these have produced excellent results for hundreds of users.

Just as you did with the primer, you'll need to decide what kind of paint you want to use on the tractor. While some restorers prefer acrylic enamel, others opt for the new polyurethane finishes.

According to Jim Seward, a tractor restorer from Wellman, Iowa, who manages the body shop for a General Motors dealership as a career, basically three types of paint are in use today. These include "implement" or synthetic enamel, acrylic enamel, and urethane as a single-stage top coat or base coat/clear coat. Although lacquer was often used in the past, Seward and other tractor restorers say it is pretty much a thing of the past.

Implement or Synthetic Enamel Paints

Seward describes implement enamel paints as anything that comes in a can from the equipment dealership or farm store. This includes aerosol cans of red, black, or cream-colored paint used to touch up parts. That doesn't mean these paints are a poor choice, though. There are literally hundreds of Farmall tractors in the country that have been restored with No. 2150 red paint purchased through the Case IH dealership. And you'll find just as many John Deere tractors painted with Classic Green enamel purchased from the John Deere dealership.

Over the years, literally hundreds of Farmall tractors have been painted with No. 2150 red paint purchased from the Case IH dealer.

One advantage of implement enamel purchased from the farm equipment dealership is that spray cans of paint—which precisely match the canned paint—are available for touch-up.

"The one good thing about these is the price," Seward says. "They're a lot less expensive than either the acrylic enamel or a base coat/clear coat. Unfortunately, they don't have near as much gloss, and the chemical bond often isn't as good."

Acrylic Enamel Paints

Perhaps the most popular paint type these days is acrylic enamel since it is available in a broad range of colors, allowing it to be custom mixed to match virtually any tractor color. In addition, enamel is relatively forgiving and requires minimal surface preparation. The downside is it takes a little longer to dry and must be applied in multiple, light coats to keep it from running. It also costs about twice as much as implement enamel.

According to Gary Ledford, a paint technician from St. Joseph, Missouri, another characteristic of acrylic enamel is that it dries from the outside in. This means that the underneath side of the coat

Although acrylic enamel is one option for those who need to duplicate a specific tractor color, most automotive supply stores have moved on to acrylic lacquers and urethane finishes.

is still porous for quite some time. As a result, if you spray back over it too soon, the new coat will work its way under the top layer and cause it to lift or wrinkle. Remember, unlike lacquer—which air dries—enamel paints dry and adhere through a chemical process.

For that reason, both he and Seward recommend the use of a hardener, which causes the coat to dry from the inside out and allows recoats without a lift problem. With a hardener, the next coat can be applied as soon as the first coat is dry to the touch. In addition, an acrylic hardener will increase the gloss and provide a more durable finish. Adding a hardener has the negative effect, though, of reducing the pot life of the mixed paint. In the case of enamel, the pot life goes from about 24 hours without hardener to about four hours once the hardener has been added.

Urethane Paints

Urethane paints, which are actually part of the enamel family, are becoming popular for tractor restoration, as well. Among the reasons are the fast drying time compared to acrylic enamel and the durability and luster that accompany the hard finish. On the other hand, urethane paints are not available in nearly as many colors as acrylic enamels.

Ledford notes that there are basically two types of urethane in use. Perhaps the most common is single-stage urethane. Like acrylic enamels, single-stage urethanes don't need to be clear coated, although both single-stage urethanes and acrylic

Urethane clear coat is applied in the same manner as you would apply paint. That includes the use of a reducer and hardener. You just have to watch more carefully for runs, since it goes on clear.

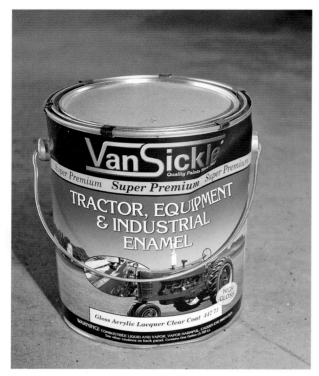

Jim Deardorff, owner of Superior Coatings in Chillicothe, Missouri, has been testing an acrylic lacquer clear coat from Van Sickle Paint Company with good success.

Deardorff often performs his own tests on different finishes and paint products by shooting them onto scrap panels and leaving them exposed to the elements.

enamels can be clear coated for additional shine and protection. In the absence of a clear coat, at least three coats of single-stage urethane are generally recommended.

The other type of urethane finish is a base coat with a clear-coat finish, which is what most of the automotive manufacturers use on all new vehicles. In effect, less pigment can often be used to lay down a color, and the gloss comes from the clear coats that go over it. As a result, base-coat finishes require at least two to three coats of clear coat for both protection and shine. Still, Ledford generally recommends three coats of base color and a minimum of two clear coats.

"The one thing about a base-coat/clear-coat finish is it's easier to correct mistakes than it is with a solid coating," Ledford says. "If you get a run or some other imperfection, you can just wait for it to dry, sand out the mistake, hit the area with another light coat of color to cover the area, and clear coat the entire panel. As long as the color coat is smooth and even, you're ready to go on since the gloss comes from the clear coat."

Ledford cautions, however, that you need to allow enough time for the last color coat to dry completely before starting on the clear coat. Since the reducer in the mixture basically evaporates as the paint dries, the reducer needs to be completely gone before the clear coat goes on. If it is not, you can end up with what is referred to as "solvent pop" in the clear coat—essentially, little bubbles formed by leftover reducer vapors trying to escape through the clear sealer.

Ledford says he has often seen tractor restorers use different paint types on the same tractor, too. Generally, they'll start with a single-stage urethane on the frame or engine, then switch to a base coat/clear coat on the sheet metal.

In Seward's opinion a base coat followed by a clear coat provides the best gloss of any paint coat. It's also one of the most expensive options, which means it's often reserved for museum-quality restorations. Unfortunately, a base-coat/clear-coat finish is also very susceptible to scratches, he insists.

"You wouldn't want to just take a rag to a tractor that's been collecting dust at a tractor show," he says. "You'd see hundreds of tiny scratches in the clear coat the next time you looked across the hood in the sunlight."

Most of the major automotive paint suppliers, including DuPont and Akzo Nobel, have different grades of paint, even within the polyurethane line. In this case U-Tech is the most inexpensive with Sikkens priced beyond the range of most tractor restorers.

A better alternative, he believes, is to wet sand a coat of acrylic enamel and buff it with polishing compound. "You can get nearly the same amount of gloss," he says. "It's just a lot more work, and you have all the edges to contend with."

Jeff Gravert, a full-time tractor restorer from Clay Center, Nebraska, agrees, noting, "Wet sanding and buffing may take a little bit off the depth of the paint layer, but they take out any flaws and get rid of any imperfections."

The one thing you won't get an argument about, though, is the durability of a urethane finish. According to everyone who has used urethane compared to acrylic, the former is more resistant to both fading and chipping, yet it's nearly as easy to apply as acrylic enamel.

Select the Appropriate Grade

Once you've decided on a certain type of paint, it's important to note that some of them also come in different grades. This is particularly true of urethane coatings available through professional paint suppliers like PPG, Martin-Senour, and DuPont.

According to Gary Ledford, who has extensive experience with Akzo Nobel coatings, his supplier has three different brands of automotive paint. The least expensive is U-Tech, which was initially formulated for the fleet coatings market. At around $23 per quart, it's also the most commonly used for tractor refinishing because it combines the durability of a urethane finish with a reasonable price.

The next step up is Lesonal, which runs around $86 per quart. Due to the available color matches, it's most often used for automotive repair by body shops. The top-of-the-line, meanwhile, is Sikkens, which can run as much as $150 per quart. Not surprisingly, Ledford says he can't think of any tractor restorers who have ever purchased Sikkens for a tractor restoration.

Akzo Nobel dealers aren't the only ones to offer several choices. PPG, for example, offers three different levels of paint quality marketed under the brand names Deltron, Delstar, and Omni. DuPont and Martin-Senour, of course, have their own brands and quality levels. Again, the ultimate choice is up to you. Any way you go—including the lowest-price choice—will generally be a higher quality paint than regular implement enamel.

CHAPTER 9

PAINT COLOR SELECTION

If there was ever a topic of discussion and debate among tractor restoration enthusiasts, it's paint color. Sure, it's easy to say that an Oliver tractor is green and an Allis-Chalmers tractor is orange, but the real debate comes when you question which shade of green or orange. With little exception, most of the manufacturers changed the color tint two or three times over the history of the brand.

There's an equal amount of debate, too, about the color of the trim, wheels, etc. Some companies made a change between models or between model years. Other companies switched from one color or shade to another with less planning . . . like when they ran out of paint in one color. This undoubtedly occurred even more often during the war years when supplies were tight.

For these reasons, don't assume you can go to the implement store or a farm supply and get the correct paint color. Granted, the farm and ranch supply outlet may have cans of paint labeled International Harvester Red or Allis-Chalmers

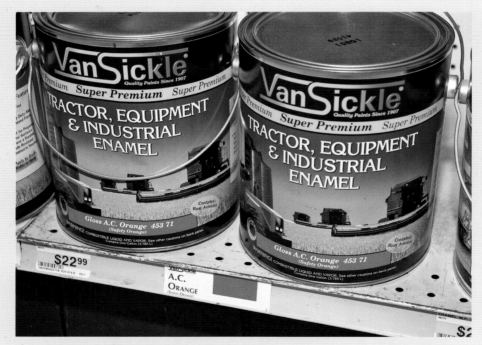

If you're striving for authenticity, you may want to avoid implement enamel paints that are simply labeled Ford Gray or Allis-Chalmers Orange because several companies changed the color tint over the years.

Although Allis-Chalmers tractors have been orange since 1929, the color tint of the Persian Orange changed three times before the company was sold in 1985.

Case tractors changed from gray to Flambeau Red, which actually looks closer to orange, in 1939. Later, the sheet metal changed to Desert Sunset while the cast components remained Flambeau Red.

Orange, but they may or may not be an exact match to the paint color originally used on your tractor. Canned paint can also vary in color from one can to the next. Because of this, these paints are generally best left to farmers who want to touch up their work tractors. If you're going for a true restoration, it's best to purchase an enamel product formulated by the manufacturer or go with automotive paint and have it custom mixed to the true color.

The bottom line, as most people will tell you, is that you should paint your tractor the shade and color that makes you happy. In the meantime, consider the history of the following brands and their different paint schemes as a starting point.

Allis-Chalmers

Beginning with the first tractor the company produced in 1914, Allis-Chalmers painted all of its early tractors with a shade of green that is today best replicated by DuPont No. 2619D. The company switched to its infamous Persian Orange color in 1929—supposedly after Harry Merritt, manager of the tractor division at the time, saw a field of brilliant orange poppies while on a trip to California. Of course, that's just one story concerning the origin of the paint color.

Allis-Chalmers changed the original Persian Orange to a more brilliant shade in 1960 and called

it Persian Orange No 2. The tractor line was also highlighted with cream-colored wheels, grilles, steering wheels, and nameplates. So it's important to know the model year of your tractor if you want to keep the paint color authentic. At practically every tractor show, true Allis-Chalmers enthusiasts will find a tractor that carries the wrong shade of Persian Orange for the model year.

Case

Tractors were nothing new to Case in the early 1900s, when farm tractors were really coming of age. The company had already become the largest producer of steam engines between 1870 and 1925. Naturally, it continued using most of the same colors, which meant its first tractors were dark green followed by gray.

The colorful change from gray to Flambeau Red came in 1939, which was around the same time that other tractor manufacturers opted for brighter colors. That was also the same year Case introduced new styling on models like the D and the R; however, the color changed again in 1957 when Case introduced the Desert Sunset paint scheme. While the cast iron remained Flambeau Red, the lighter color dominated the sheet metal, including the hood and fenders.

Cockshutt

Founded as a company in 1877, Cockshutt got its start in the tractor business in 1924 by marketing Hart-Parr tractors with red and cream paint and the Cockshutt name on the radiator shell.

Following World War II, Cockshutt finally had the resources to come out with its own tractor, the Model 30, in 1946. Naturally, it continued the red-and-yellow paint scheme as a Cockshutt model. The same tractor was also sold in the United States as the Co-Op E3 by the National Farm Machinery Cooperative, based in Ohio, and as the Farmcrest tractor through the American Gambles Stores chain. During their reign, the Co-op tractors supposedly carried at least two different shades of orange, with the latest represented by Martin-Senour No. 90T-22014.

Imports from Canada, Cockshutt tractors carried some version of red and cream paint until the 1950s when the Deluxe models were introduced with red and yellow paint. In 1958, Cockshutt switched to a Harvest Gold paint scheme.

In the meantime, Cockshutt continued with the red and yellow paint scheme until the early 1950s, when the Deluxe models were introduced. At that time, the color of the hood, grille, and fuel tank was changed to a cream color, while the rest of the tractor remained red. Finally, in 1958, Cockshutt debuted the new 500 Series with a new squared-off grille and an all-yellow paint scheme called Harvest Gold.

A few years later, in 1961, the "red belly" paint scheme came into play, which featured a Vermillion Red transmission, engine, and frame to contrast the Harvest Gold sheet metal.

Farmall/International Harvester

Like most other tractor brands, IH started painting its first tractors with a drab color—Tractor Gray, as the company called it—that seemed to match the times. In November 1936, International Harvester made the change to Farmall Red for its 1937 models.

Although the red color remained the same over the years, Farmall and McCormick tractors did go through a number of changes in trim colors, which included cream, blue, and black. Wheels, meanwhile, were either red or galvanized; most restorers reproduce the galvanized look with silver paint.

As you'll discover in the chapter on decals, International Harvester also complicated the paint issue with a program in the 1950s in which customers could have the local dealer repaint their tractors. In many of these cases, employees at the dealership weren't as careful about masking off certain parts as the factory workers had been. For example, on Letter Series tractors, such as the M, C, and H, engineering specifications called for leaving electronic components unpainted. This included the magneto, spark plugs, coil wires, and, in most cases, the distributor cover. It's not uncommon, however, to see many of these parts painted red today—especially the distributor cap and some wires.

If you really want to do your research on the correct paint scheme, you might want to go to the Wisconsin Historical Society website (www.wisconsinhistory.org) and search through its library of documents from IH. All of the IH paint committee decisions from 1924 through 1960 are listed on the site.

If, for instance, you have a 1931 F-20, you'll discover in a paint committee memo dated June 5, 1930, that the drawbar on Farmall tractors was to be painted Harvest Red instead of Tractor Gray as it originally had been. The decision was made at the request of the works manager, who stated that "because of the physical layout of the Farmall equipment," some money could be saved by painting the drawbar the same color as the wheels. The trunnion castings and braces were to remain gray, as in the past; however, if you look around at many tractor shows, most Farmall tractors continue to have a gray drawbar, regardless of the year.

Another memo, dated September 24, 1946, states that all tractor weights are to be painted the same color as the tractor. No notation is made as to what color they were previously.

Until the company introduced its 1937 models in 1936, most Farmall and International Harvester tractors were painted Tractor Gray.

International Harvester tractors are easily recognized today by their bright Harvest Red paint coat. In fact, about the only thing in their paint scheme that has changed since 1937 has been the trim color.

Ferguson

After dissolving his partnership with Henry Ford, Harry Ferguson continued to build and market his own brand of tractors from 1948 until 1953, when Massey-Harris acquired the Ferguson company and renamed the company Massey-Harris-Ferguson. To keep the company afloat after Ford split on the agreement, Ferguson imported tractors from Europe as the TE-20. Then, in 1951, Ferguson introduced the TO-20, which was produced specifically for the American market. Other tractors that followed included the TO-30 and TO-35.

In an effort to build on the reputation that had been established by the Ford-Ferguson 9N and 2N models, the Ferguson tractors continued to use an all-gray paint scheme for a few years. In fact, one of the company's early ads proclaimed, "Fortunate is the Dealer who offers the all-gray tractor with the Chevron Nameplate."

Although the gray color looks very similar to the solid gray on Ford 9N and 2N models, it does have a different paint code number, which is referred to as Ferguson Gray. However, in 1954, Ferguson switched to a Ferguson Light Gray paint

All Ford tractors were painted solid gray until 1948, when Ford split from Ferguson and introduced the 8N with its red and gray paint scheme.

Whether it's because the previous owners wanted their tractor to look like an 8N, you'll find more 9N and 2N tractors that are painted red and gray than those painted only gray.

This Ford 8N, beautifully restored by Chris Mercer with some help from his father, Dallas, shows the true colors for a Model 8N. *Chris Mercer*

Later-model Ford tractors carried various color schemes of the red and gray until the colors were changed to blue and gray in 1964.

on the TO-35 with yellow-green metallic on the TO-35 castings and F-40 grille screen panels.

The company changed paint color again in 1956 when Old MF Red or Tractor Red was used on the sheet metal on the TO-35s and the F-40 grille screen panels. A Flint Gray Metallic, meanwhile, was used on the castings of TO-35 and F-40 models, giving rise to the red and gray paint scheme that followed with Massey Ferguson.

Ford

It doesn't take much planning to paint a Ford 9N tractor, which made its debut in 1939, or a Model 2N, which followed in 1942. It just takes the right shade of gray paint, since the entire tractor, including the wheels and frame, are all the same color on both models. Although the Ford Motor Company generally gets most of the credit for the 9N and the 2N, the first two N Series models were actually the result of a partnership between Henry Ford and Harry Ferguson.

Unfortunately, that partnership dissolved in 1946, and by 1947, it was clear that each of them was going in his own direction—especially when Ford introduced the 8N with its distinctive red castings and wheels. The rest of the 8N was painted a lighter gray than the previous 2N and 9N models. Even after Ford introduced several larger tractors, including the NAA, 600, and 861 Powermaster, the company continued to use a mix of red and gray

paint. The only difference was that a few models, like the 601, used more red than gray.

The paint scheme changed completely, though, in 1958, when Ford introduced a new line of tractors that included the Model 5000. At that point, Ford introduced the famous blue color that was recognized until the company was purchased by New Holland.

Although there are a number of sources that carry both the dark gray and the lighter gray introduced on the 8N, the biggest debate today centers around which shade of gray is correct. Many claim, for example, that several brands or paint codes specified for the 8N are too white, while other paint codes have too much of a tan or beige tint.

John Deere

John Deere tractors are unique in the vintage tractor world in that they have always been green and yellow, unless of course you're restoring an industrial model. If you're going for a true restoration, you have a couple of choices. One is to go to an automotive paint supplier and have the paint custom mixed to the true color. The other is to go to the John Deere dealership for your supplies. Keep in mind, though, that John Deere changed the shade of green around the time it introduced its New Generation tractors, which included the 3010, 4010, etc., in 1960. If you shop for paint at the dealership, you'll find it has two Deere shades: Agricultural Green and

As one of the most recognized tractor brands today, John Deere tractors have been green and yellow since the day the company introduced the Waterloo Boy in 1918.

Although the difference is subtle, vintage John Deere tractors were painted with what is today called Classic Green paint, while newer tractors carry an Agricultural Green paint coat.

While a number of manufacturers offered industrial tractors, they were almost always painted a different color than the companies' agricultural tractors.

It was in 1938 that Massey-Harris switched from gray paint to the Radiant Red and Straw Yellow paint scheme that has since become associated with Massey tractors.

Classic Green. The latter is primarily used on two-cylinder models.

According to technical representatives for the Two-Cylinder Club, nearly 80 percent of the tractors at John Deere expos have John Deere–brand paint. On the other hand, Dan Peterson, with Rusty Acres Restoration, says he prefers a regular acrylic enamel, specifically a product produced by Martin-Senour.

Massey-Harris/Massey Ferguson

Although the first Massey-Harris Challenger tractors were painted gray, most of us know Massey as the brand that sported Radiant Red paint with Straw Yellow wheels. In fact, that trend actually started with the Challenger, following its restyling around 1938. It continued until 1955, which was shortly after the merger of Harry Ferguson's tractor company with Massey-Harris.

Under Massey-Harris-Ferguson, new sheet metal and a new red and gray paint scheme were introduced on the MF-35. Eventually, the "Harris" portion of the name was dropped. As a division of AGCO Corporation, Massey Ferguson continues to build tractors today with the familiar red and gray paint scheme.

Minneapolis-Moline

According to Minneapolis-Moline enthusiasts, M-M used three recognized shades of Prairie Gold paint on the tractors the company manufactured from 1936 to 1963. Prior to that, the brand was known as Twin City and carried a shade of gray.

In general, it is believed that M-M used the original Prairie Gold for only two years—from 1936 to perhaps as late as 1938. At that time, the company switched to Prairie Gold No. 2, which was used from 1938 (some say 1939) until 1955 (and until 1959 on the GB models). The biggest question when it comes to paint shade concerns the 1938 ZT, GT, and UT, which some say used the original Prairie Gold and others believe were painted with Prairie Gold No. 2.

In 1956, Minneapolis-Moline made another paint change to Power Yellow, sometimes referred to as Late Prairie Gold. Although the tint is very close to Prairie Gold No. 2, it does have a little more of an orange tint (hence the designation by some as Orange Prairie Gold). This color was primarily used on all Powerline models built from 1956 to 1961 and on the early 335, 445, Four State, Four Star Super, M5, M-504, GVI, and G-704 models built through 1962 and 1963.

Finally, in 1962 or 1963, M-M switched to an Energy Yellow paint, which is sometimes referred to as an industrial yellow. Models painted this color include the G-705 and G-706.

Like most brands, the trim colors were another story. In general, the Prairie Gold tractors all carried Cherry Red trim and wheels. However, things began to take a twist in 1959, when the entire Jet Star tractor was painted Metallic Brown with wheels trimmed in Power Yellow. The rest of the tractors were painted Power Yellow with a Metallic Brown frame. In addition, the hood on the M5, M-504, GVI, and G-704 tractors had a dark maroon-red accent stripe and the wheels were painted Power Yellow. If the tractor was equipped with power adjustable wheels, though, the rims were silver.

According to most sources, M-M also used two different brown colors during the later years. The early Four Star, Four Star Super, M5, M-504, GVI, and G-704 used the same metallic brown color used on the Jet Star. Then around 1963, supposedly at the same time M-M switched to Energy Yellow,

Minneapolis-Moline first introduced its Prairie Gold paint color in 1936, shortly after acquiring the Twin City tractor line.

This lineup of Minneapolis-Moline tractors shows the transition from Prairie Gold to Prairie Gold No. 2 to Energy Yellow. Note how the trim color also changed over the years.

the change was made to Dyna Brown. Basically, this means that Metallic Brown goes with Power Yellow and Dyna Brown goes with Energy Yellow.

That doesn't mean that rule is set in stone, however. Most likely, the company used up existing supplies before making the switch on a few models. As a final change, M-M dropped the Dyna Brown in favor of white in 1967 and continued that trend until 1970. As a result, the paint scheme consisted of a yellow and white two-tone hood with a black trim band, and the fenders and cast metal were Energy Yellow.

In the 1970s, some wheels were white with silver rims—most likely from the Oliver influence.

That's because M-M was purchased by White Motor Company in 1963 as a sister brand to Oliver Farm Equipment Corporation, which was purchased in 1960, and Cockshutt Farm Equipment Corporation, which was acquired in 1962. That, of course, led to a whole series of crossover models that were simply painted different colors.

As a result, any models produced after 1970 often shared colors with White, Oliver, and/or Cockshutt, which means that, yes, there were even a few red and white Minneapolis-Moline tractors. But that's a subject perhaps best left to a brand-specific publication. Besides, the 1970s are really getting beyond the scope of vintage tractors in most books.

Oliver

Oliver tractors came about as the result of a merger of five related companies in 1929 under the umbrella of Oliver Farm Equipment Corporation. One of those,

of course, was the Hart-Parr Company, which built the first farm tractor in 1903. With this head start, Oliver Hart-Parr introduced its Model 18/28 in 1930, setting the stage for green tractors with red wheels.

Like a few other brands, though, Oliver went through several changes in the shade of the color used over the years. According to Lyle Dumont—an Oliver collector from Sigorney, Iowa, and a partner in the Oliver Decals business with his wife, Helen— Oliver used as many as four different shades of green from 1930 through 1975, when the company became part of White. Unfortunately, he says, there aren't any records that specify exact colors on specific models, which has forced him and other collectors to locate old paint codes and compare current paint numbers to pieces taken off the tractors.

Another problem, he says, is you can talk to 10 different people and get close to 10 different answers for paint color. The Martin-Senour numbers listed

For a while, Oliver continued to use the dark green color on its tractors that was previously used on the Hart-Parr brand (foreground) the company acquired.

Like several other companies, Oliver went through a series of color shades over the years, even though the main color always remained green.

on the chart at the end of this chapter are the closest that Dumont has been able to come by matching actual sheetmetal panels with the paint chips.

Dumont says Oliver started with a dark green, which is essentially the same color used on Hart-Parr tractors. When the company came out with the four- and six-cylinder engines around 1935 to 1936, however, it switched to a lighter green. The color went to an even lighter shade around 1939, when Oliver came out with the styled models that included the 60 and 70. The shade was lightened again when the company introduced the Fleetline Series. The final change came when Oliver introduced the Super Series.

According to some, there was one more change with the 55 Series, but Dumont says he has never seen much difference in the color after the Super Series.

In the meantime, trim colors consisted of yellow with red highlights followed by Clover White on later models. Dumont cautions, however, that even though there is a touch of green in the Clover White formulation, some colors go too heavy on the green, which looks unnatural.

Available Colors

As mentioned earlier, tractor paint is available from a wide range of sources, including the local hardware or farm supply store. As most collectors will tell you, though, those aren't the best sources for a quality paint job. The better option, they say, is to

One of the last color schemes used on Oliver tractors was a light shade of green with Clover White trim.

purchase your supplies from an automotive paint supplier. Most of them have paint codes for the major tractor brands; however, what they call Allis-Chalmers Orange could be Persian Orange No. 1 or it could be No. 2.

Valspar, for example, has a line of enamel called Restoration Series Tractor and Implement Finish, which is available in eight "classic colors." The colors include JD Green, Ford Gray, MF Red, AC Orange, JD Yellow, Ford Red, IH Red, and Ford Blue. Unfortunately, like the implement paint label at the farm supply store, the brochure doesn't specify a

Don't judge correct tractor color by what you observe at a tractor auction or even by the color of the tractor before you stripped the paint. Case tractors were never as yellow as the one at top, and Ford tractors weren't painted blue until 1964, which was well after this Model 9N (above) was introduced.

shade. Perhaps the dealer has more information, but the paint chip on the Ford Gray, for example, looks more like the 8N gray than the 2N or 9N shade.

If you want to get a more specific or exact shade, you have a couple of options. One is to start with the paint codes listed in this chapter. These have been compiled from a number of sources, including paint color books, paint code charts posted on the internet, and discussion boards on various tractor websites. Still, there is no guarantee of accuracy here. It's worth noting, however, that in many cases, more than one source agreed on a color. At least three different sources, for example, agreed that PPG's No. 60080 is a very close match to Allis-Chalmer's Persian Orange No. 1.

You'll also note that paint codes are supplied for five different suppliers. Dupont and PPG seem to be the predominant sources for most tractor restorers, as indicated by the number of available codes from those two suppliers. But others prefer Martin-Senour (NAPA), TISCO, and Sherwin-Williams. Those numbers are supplied in cases where they were available.

Keep in mind that most paint suppliers can cross-reference their number to that of another company. So if you at least have one number as a starting point, you can usually find what you're looking for. That doesn't mean you will have an exact match, though. According to several tractor restorers, one company's paint color may not match another company's color, even though they use the same number to cross-reference the shade.

With the advanced technology available today, tractor restorers have yet another option for selecting paint color. That is to have your paint supplier use a computer-based machine called a "color eye" or color spectrometer to determine the color. Not every paint outlet will have one, of course. But if you can find a professional paint store that does, it's simply a matter of finding a piece of sheet metal that hasn't faded over the years and having the technician take a color-reading scan. This information is then downloaded to a computer, which interprets the color and displays the appropriate paint formula. This is especially valuable when

The best resources for determining the original colors of the various components are vintage photographs found in tractor ads or literature, since other restorers have occasionally been wrong.

painting an orphan tractor or early model for which paint codes aren't available. Although the paint matching process can't always be 100 percent accurate, it does tend to be very accurate on single-stage paints.

Some places to check for original paint color are on the underside of the fuel tank or hood or on the backside of a mounting bracket. You may want to use some polishing compound on the area to remove oxidation, but if the area has been protected from exposure, it should be pretty close to original. Even without the use of a color spectrometer,

Virtually any color you could ever need can be mixed with the toners stocked by automotive paint stores and many body shops. Custom paint mixing is done by weight (note the scales on the far left) as the base and different amounts of toner are weighed out one at a time.

an unfaded paint sample will give you something to compare paint chips to when shopping for the color coat.

As a final hint on tractor painting, it may be helpful to check out some of the websites maintained by individual tractor enthusiasts and a number of tractor clubs. The paint color data on some websites goes so far as to tell you which parts of the engine are painted and what the correct color should be. One of the most common questions, for instance, is whether the exhaust manifold should be painted and, if so, what color. Often, the radiator fan on various brands and models was painted different colors over the years. Sometimes it was black or painted to match the engine, and sometimes it was painted a color that made it more visible for safety reasons.

Of course, all this only matters if you're interested in complete accuracy in an attempt to restore a tractor to its original appearance. If you're painting a work tractor or a pulling tractor, it probably doesn't make any difference to anyone.

If you're striving for an authentic look, you need to know which parts of the tractor were painted different colors. Some painters, for example, might assume the fan on a John Deere two-cylinder tractor would be painted the same color as the engine. Instead, it's painted yellow, undoubtedly to make it more visible when the engine is running.

Paint Color Codes

Below is a listing of the most commonly sought-out paint colors and various paint suppliers' shade codes for them:

	DuPont	TISCO	PPG	Martin Senour	Sherwin-Williams
Allis-Chalmers					
Persian Orange 1	655	TP280	60080	99L3723	
Persian Orange 2			60396		
A-C Orange	29047		60691	90T-3723	
Yellow	421		81330		
Cream		TP270	8638		
Green	2619D	TP380			
Case					
Gray	24938		32678		
Green	262				
Black	93-005		9000		
Flambeau Red	016DH	TP140	70138	99L3724	
Desert Sunset		TP580	81357		
Power Red	G8156 UAD	TP890			
Caterpillar					
Cat Yellow	H7947 D	TP170	80021		
Highway Yellow	421		80979		
Cletrac					
Orange	017 D		60045	90T-3728	
Green	GS380				
Cockshutt					
Red			78210	99-23797-0	JK8522-G
Yellow			88234		JK6475
Harvest Gold			83761		JK8523
Co-Op					
Late Orange				90T-22014	
Ford					
Modern Dark Blue	29509		12908		
Ford Gray	29665		31657		
Empire Blue	27863D	TP360			
Industrial Yellow		TP760			
Light Gray		TP330		99L3732	
Medium Gray		TP240			
Red	RS465	TP310	70075	99L4338	

	DuPont	TISCO	PPG	Martin Senour	Sherwin-Williams
Ferguson					
Gray (1946-54)	652		32676	10039	1337
Light Gray (54-56)	N9650		33965	3740	4030
Yellow-Green	B9533		47383	2245	11558
Tractor Red (56-60)	7505	70738	4763	7191	
Flint Gray Metallic	L7949		34690	3746	4650
Bamboo Beige	L8071		25035	22986	32145
Hart-Parr					
1918–19 Green				99L8753	
1928–29 Green				99L8747	
1929–37 Green				99L11513	
International Harvester					
IH Gray	98620				
IH Green	93-84155				
IH Red	7410 D	TP1101	71310		
IH White	24440	TP900			
Blue	24160		10067		
Cub Cadet Yellow	79535 D		81518		
Cub Cadet White	57350 A		8665		
John Deere					
Green	262 D	TP210	46180		
Yellow	263 D	TP190	80186		
Industrial Yellow	43007 D	TP530	82295		
Massey Ferguson					
Red	77932 D	TP300	72598		
Tractor Red			70837		
Gray	652	TP230			
Metallic Flint Gray	LM447	TP320	31644		
Silver Mist Gray	83825 D	TP750	31991		
Industrial Yellow		TP540	81518		
Massey-Harris					
Red	27958 D		70364	99-4354	
Straw Yellow	3274		80533	99-4341	
Bronze	B8191				

	DuPont	TISCO	PPG	Martin Senour	Sherwin-Williams
Minneapolis-Moline					
Prairie Gold	006 D		60098		
Prairie Gold 2	020DH		60039	99L3749	
Industrial Yellow	K9590AK				
M-M Red			71528	90G540	
M-M Cherry Red			70385	99G540	
Metallic Brown	C8194AH				
Dyna Brown			22394		
Dyna Brown 2			23049		
Oliver					
Dark Green	0149 or 030	TP220	99L8758		
Lighter Green				99L11513	
Styled Tractor Green			99L8748		
Fleetline Green	1317			99L8746	
Fleetline/Super Green	GS911		99L3751		
Yellow	44087			99L11611	
Red (wheels)	M9218			99L3752	
Clover White	4775		DAR46536		
Silver King					
Silver	5476A				
Twin City (M-M)					
Gray			31953		
White					
Blue	G8164			12773	
Orange				2235	
Red				72231	

CHAPTER 10

PRIMER AND PAINT APPLICATION

If you're doing a paint job as part of a restoration, you probably can't wait to get the tractor assembled and get started painting. But try to restrain yourself just a little longer. You'll achieve the best results and have the easiest time painting your tractor if it is still disassembled. That means you should look at priming and painting individual sections of sheet metal, as well as the frame and engine, separately.

By leaving as many parts off the tractor as possible, you also have the opportunity to paint both sides of a piece in one session. Components like the seat, grille, battery box, and instrument panel can be hung on wire hooks, for example, and coated on all surfaces, without having to let one side dry first.

Using the hood from a Farmall tractor as a demonstration panel, Jim Seward, a tractor restorer from Wellman, Iowa, shows the transition (right to left) from original finish through bare metal with some filler, etch primer, epoxy primer, sealer, base-coat paint, and clear coat.

Painting a tractor is also much easier if you have room to spread out the parts and paint them individually before trying to assemble them into a finished project.

Hanging small parts on coat hangers or pieces of wire allows you to paint all sides of the part in one pass. It also allows you to get parts up on a level where you can keep the gun on a horizontal plane.

One trick that saves a lot of hand painting is to push fasteners into a piece of cardboard or to insert them into holes drilled in a board. This lets you spray paint all the bolt heads of a like color in one pass.

Because they have the tractors custom painted off the premises, the staff members at N-Complete built a set of carts to haul the remanufactured chassis between the facility and the nearby paint shop. This also allows the painter to move around and under the frame without obstruction.

Also know that the safety precautions and application techniques that apply to painting also apply to the primer coat (which you should complete first). So now that you know about the different types of primers and paint, here's a look at how to apply them.

Fire Safety First

As you're setting up shop and getting ready to paint, remember that paint, thinners, and solvents are highly flammable, particularly when atomized by an air-powered spray gun. So be sure the area is free of any open sources of ignition, and keep a fire extinguisher nearby. Some additional safety precautions provided by PPG include:

- Make sure paints, solvents, and other flammable liquids are safely stored in a secure area.
- The quantity of flammable liquids stored in the spraying area should not exceed what is required for one day's use.
- Paint and solvent products should be kept away from all sources of ignition, including heat, sparks, flames, motors, burners, heaters, pilot lights, and welding.
- Paint- or solvent-soaked rags should be replaced frequently.
- Be sure the filtration system is clean at all times.
- Check frequently to ensure that the exhaust system is operating efficiently.
- Be aware that the high pressure of airless spraying can inject coatings into the skin, which can cause serious injury requiring immediate medical treatment.
- Never smoke or allow smoking in the painting area.

Practice Makes Perfect

If you haven't done much painting in the past, the first step should be to find an old tractor fender or a sheet of plywood and practice your application technique. Read through the following procedures on adjusting and using the paint gun and then simply practice.

Also, use a can of inexpensive paint to get a feel for holding the gun on vertical and horizontal

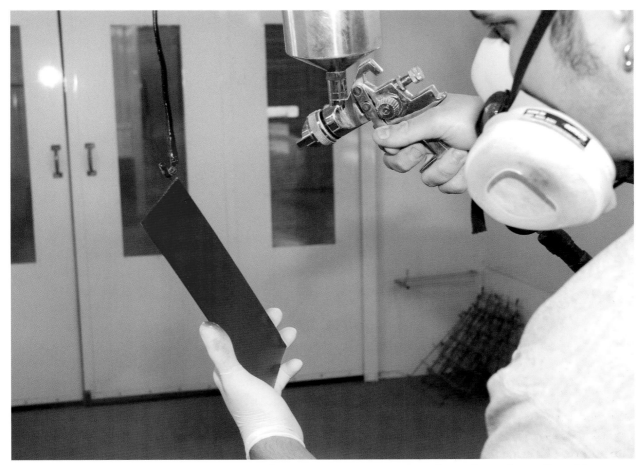

Before you start painting on the tractor, test the spray pattern on a scrap of metal or a sheet of masking paper. You want a uniform oval pattern at a distance of 8 to 12 inches.

surfaces. Then adjust the paint volume and pattern adjustment knobs and see what kind of difference it makes. Use the spray gun air cap to adjust the spray pattern orientation from horizontal to vertical or vice versa. Learn how to overlap each pass with the gun to obtain a happy medium between thin spots and runs caused by too much paint. Once you've become proficient on your practice panel, you can be assured you'll do a better job on the actual application.

Paint Mixing

Whether you're using implement enamel from the farm equipment dealership or you had paint professionally mixed by the NAPA dealer or automotive paint store, you should have a container of paint that is ready to go as soon as you open the can.

When painting a tractor, it's important that you use a thinner or reducer to obtain the correct consistency. Several thin coats are better than one or two thick ones. Adding a hardener, to improve drying time and strengthen the paint coat, is also a good idea.

Most reducers come in three different speeds, which is based on temperature range of the work area and the size of the job—slow, medium, and fast. Since reducers and thinners act as carriers that evaporate as the paint cures, the speed is basically the evaporation speed. Consequently, you'll note that each speed has a temperature range. In general, fast reducers are designed for cooler temperatures and slow reducers are for use in higher temperatures. Using a fast reducer in 90-degree weather can cause the paint to dry too fast for the job, and using a cool temperature reducer in an extremely warm shop can cause paint to blush, fade, or cause other problems.

The paint won't be your only ingredient, though. You'll also need to mix in the reducer or thinner to dilute it to a sprayable liquid and improve the spray pattern. You'll need to follow the specifications provided by the paint label or your paint supplier, but you can generally figure on something close to a one-to-one ratio of paint or primer to thinner or reducer.

Your paint supplier will tell you that thinners and reducers do basically the same thing and that they're usually referred to as thinners when used with lacquers and reducers when used with enamels, including urethane products. While they may do the same thing, they're certainly not the same product. You may remember using paint thinner to clean brushes or fix mistakes with glue or paint. Paint reducers, on the other hand, are formulated specifically for acrylic enamels and urethanes and don't offer crossover applications. Reducers also come in different speeds to match the size of the job and the temperature. Again, your paint supplier can help you determine the correct "speed" of reducer for your needs.

Whatever you do, don't use gasoline in place of a reducer or thinner, even though some people have done so. It's not safe, and any money you save won't be worth the risk to the quality of the end product, not to mention risking your own safety.

In addition, you'll need to add a specific amount of hardener to the products, assuming your

Sikkens

AKZO NOBEL

AUTOCRYL®

TECHNICAL DATA S
Page 3 of 5
June 2001

POT LIFE:	2 hours at 70°F (20°C) with Autocryl Hardener 45 minutes at 70°F (20°C) with Autocryl Hardener Rapid
NOTE:	Please see the Sikkens Standard Hardener / Activators technical data sheet more information on the pot life of Autocryl.
NOTE:	When mixing the 3:1:1 ratio, Autocryl 242, Autocryl metallic colors or colors high percentages of 00 White, an additional 5–10% Autocryl Reducer Fast m added for easier application.
SPRAY GUN & PRESSURE:	

	Fluid Tip	Spraying Pressure	Fluid Pres
Siphon Feed	0.055"–0.067" (1.4–1.7 mm)	40–50 psi (3–4 bar)	
Gravity Feed	0.051"–0.055" (1.3–1.4 mm)	40–50 psi (3–4 bar)	
Pressure Feed	0.039"–0.047" (1.0–1.2 mm)	40–50 psi (3–4 bar)	8–10 psi (0.6–0.8 ba
HVLP Siphon	0.071"–0.087" (1.8–2.2 mm)	max. 10 psi (max. 0.8 bar)	
HVLP Gravity	0.051" 2 2		

Most paint obtained from a professional paint dealer has a tech sheet that tells you everything you need to know concerning flash times, drying time, protective equipment required, pot life, required pressure, and more.

preference and if the label call for it. In addition to helping the paint dry faster, an acrylic hardener will increase the gloss and provide a more durable finish. Adding a hardener has the negative effect, though, of reducing the pot life of the mixed paint. In the case of enamel, the pot life goes from about 24 hours without hardener to about four hours once the hardener has been added. If you have any questions about the ingredients or the amounts that need to be mixed, talk to your paint supplier.

One of the easiest ways to measure and mix the paint is to use a clear mixing cup that has calibrations printed on the outside. Simply pour in the paint or primer, followed by the thinner or reducer until the liquid reaches the appropriate calibration mark for each. Do the same with the hardener. You can then use a stir stick to mix the components in the mixing cup before pouring it into the paint gun canister or gravity cup.

Paint manufacturers and their vendors also offer calibrated paint mixing sticks that work in a similar manner to the mixing cups. In this case, you can pour the paint into any straight-sided container and use the calibrated stick to measure out the appropriate amount of paint. Then add the thinner or reducer until the level on the stick hits the next

Carefully measure out the correct amount of paint, reducer, and hardener for each canister or spray cup refill. If you don't know the exact amount needed, measure each ingredient into a calibrated measuring cup and then transfer it into the gun canister. Remember, never pour any mixed paint back into the can.

appropriate mark. Add any necessary hardener in the same manner and use the stirring stick to mix the liquids together.

Once all the components have been measured and blended by either method, pour the mixture through a paint filter placed over the opening of the paint gun cup or canister. This is your last chance to prevent any impurities or clumps from entering spray gun passages and causing a clog or misspray.

Make sure the canister is securely fastened to the paint gun or the lid on a gravity-feed unit has been screwed on straight or secured, and you're ready to start painting.

Even if you thoroughly stirred the paint in the can and it appears to be free of clumps, you should pour it through a paint strainer. Foreign material can easily clog the tiny passages in the gun and negatively affect the paint job.

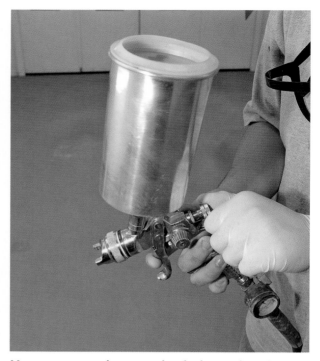

Most spray guns have two knobs located on the back of the gun housing for adjusting the paint material and airflow. The amount of material is usually controlled by the knob that is in line with the air nozzle, while airflow is controlled with the other knob. Always consult your manual for exact adjustment procedures.

Adjust the Spray Pattern

Before you start shooting paint on the tractor, it's important that you adjust both the spray mixture and the spray pattern. One, of course, can affect the other. In general, several thin coats of paint are better than one or two thick ones. On the other hand, if you get the paint too thin, it can have a dusty appearance that reduces gloss and shine.

Assuming you've created a paint/reducer mixture that sprays smoothly and evenly, adjust the nozzle to spray an oval that is approximately three inches by six inches at about one foot distance. Most guns have two control knobs on the back—one for the fan spray and the other for the volume of spray that exits the nozzle. The air pressure, meanwhile, should be adjusted at the compressor or your air filter unit. Naturally, different products and

different ratios of paint and thinner will spray differently. The best way to adjust the spray is to simply spray a small amount of paint onto a test panel or sheet of cardboard.

One of the easiest ways to set up a test area is to tape sheets of masking paper to an old sheet of plywood and set it nearby. Once the paint has dried, you can just tear off that sheet and tape on a new one. This will also let you quickly retest the pattern each time you refill the gun or if you suspect it may not be spraying an even pattern.

Paint Application

If there are two keys to paint application and paint gun maneuvering, they are smoothly moving the gun in a back-and-forth motion and holding the gun perpendicular to the surface as much as possible

Smoothly move the gun from side to side as you paint the tractor, overlapping each previous spray by about half. This is particularly important on sheet metal. On the first paint coat, it's often best to spray a light "tack" coat, especially with thin paints that can run.

Be sure to direct paint spray into all the cracks and crevices around the engine and frame. But be careful. It's easy to hold the gun in one spot too long, causing a run. While applying primer and paint, it's also important that you move any control or adjustment levers to ensure that the area behind them gets painted.

at a distance of 8 to 12 inches. Both are important to produce a smooth, even coat.

If the gun is tilted too much in relation to the surface, the spray won't be uniform, which can lead to other problems. If you can picture the spray pattern hitting the surface at an angle, you can imagine the impact. The paint on one side of the circle or oval you're spraying will go on thicker because the nozzle is closer to the surface, while the other side of the oval will be thinner because the nozzle is farther away. The same thing happens if you swing the gun in an arc as you move it back and forth. As you curve your arm at the end of the arc, you're moving the gun and especially the outer edge of the spray pattern farther from the surface.

This creates the potential for the thinner paint to dry faster than the thicker paint. Unfortunately,

if you apply the second coat, based on the drying time for the thin spots or the average, there may still be thick spots where the solvent is still evaporating, which can lead to various problems including solvent pop. The other problem is that the paint you've sprayed at the far end of an arc may be too dry by the time it hits the surface, resulting in poor adhesion or a thin coat of paint.

How and when you pull and release the trigger on the paint gun is also important. You don't want to have it simply pointing at the panel when you pull the trigger. It should be aimed off to the side and then smoothly twisted into the panel as the paint starts to spray. Keep it moving at a steady, even pace until you get to the end of the panel where you can twist it away from the panel. If you've had experience with an aerosol paint can, you'll do fine.

One or more sawhorses make a good support for painting larger tractor components like fenders, allowing you to cover the top surfaces evenly.

You'll just need to learn from experience that if you go too slow, you may leave runs in the paint and if you move too fast, you may fog the paint rather than putting down a full coat. Practice on an old panel, not the tractor hood.

Since the paint will generally be thinner on the outer edge of the pattern, try to overlap the previous pattern by one-third to two-thirds of the pattern width. When painting large areas, spray around the edges first and finish up by filling in the center.

Jim Deardorff says he also likes to go around any openings, such as those for the radiator cap or fuel fill, before moving to the main portion of engine hood. Speaking of tractor hoods, one of the best ways to paint a hood is to set it over the top of a single sawhorse. This will allow you to hit all the edges and even come up underneath the edges, whereas if you place it across two sawhorses, there will always be edges touching one or both supports.

One more tip: Always hold the hose in your free hand or drape it over your shoulder while you're moving around the tractor or sheetmetal components. You don't want the hose dragging across the wet surface. At the very least, it will smear the paint coat and it may even introduce dirt into the wet surface.

Tractor wheels can best be painted with the tires removed. Estel Theis usually places them between two secured sawhorses, which allows him to paint both the inside and outside surfaces.

Having been painted in a contrasting color to the frame, the wheels and fenders for a Ford 8N tractor are set off to the side to await the tires and final assembly.

It helps if you have room to spread out parts after they have been painted so they're easier to find when reassembling the tractor.

Taking your time to do the job right can yield a tractor that is better looking than the day it left the factory 60 years ago.

Flash Times and Recoats

Yes, your tractor paint job will require more than one coat. That is particularly true if you're using enamel. Most restorers and paint suppliers recommend at least two to three coats of paint; some even use up to five or six on sheet metal for extra durability and shine. One tractor restorer, who specializes in museum-quality restorations, applies at least seven coats of enamel on sheet metal, putting one coat on right after the other. After he finishes the last coat, he lets it cure for three or four days, then wet sands all sheet metal with 1,200-grit sandpaper, staying clear of any edges. Finally, he applies the decals and sprays clear coat over both the paint and the decals to produce a gleaming shine. Any cast parts, however, receive only paint to avoid a glossy, unnatural appearance.

Even if you use a polyurethane base coat and a clear coat, you should put at least two coats of paint on your tractor. The key is to make sure the timing between paint coats is sufficient, particularly if you're using an enamel without a hardener. That's another reason most restorers and paint specialists recommend the use of a hardener. It causes the coat to dry from the inside out and allows recoats without a lift problem. The next coat can be applied as soon as the first coat is dry to the touch.

The time required for the solvents to evaporate and the paint to cure enough for the next coat is referred to in professional circles as flash time. Basically, you can't apply additional coats until the solvents from the first coat, as well as each successive coat, have had time to evaporate. If you haven't allowed sufficient flash time, you may be trapping

Spray out cards, which are available from most paint suppliers, are handy to have when painting a solid panel. Prior to painting the tractor, spray the black and white grid with enough coats to attain full coverage. This will tell you how many coats it should take to sufficiently cover the tractor. Also, the hole in the middle of the card allows you to make a color-matching check before spraying a panel that needs to match the rest of the tractor.

When painting a tractor with two colors, such as this Oliver hood, it's vital that you carefully mask off each colored area. Most restorers also recommend that you paint the smallest color area first, which in this case is the yellow. Fortunately, sections of the grille on some models can be removed and painted separately.

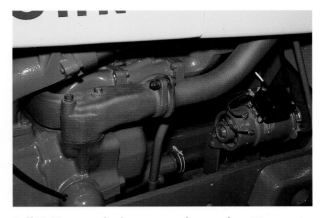

Jeff McManus, who has restored more than 70 tractors for himself and Deere and Company, likes to use a "cast gray" pigment on manifolds and rear axles.

Some restorers like to finish off the sheet metal with clear coat, while others prefer the look of hand-buffed enamel.

solvent vapors under the new coat and that can lead to blistering, cracking, lifting, sagging, or any of a number of other problems.

On the other hand, since the coats rely on a chemical bond for adhesion, you don't want to wait too long between coats either. Most paint coatings, or your paint supplier, will provide some kind of guidance, so follow those recommendations. Realize, though, that additional coats may require longer flash times than the initial coat. Some painters say they have learned to test the surface with their thumb on a hidden area. If the paint doesn't show their thumbprint, it's ready to accept the next coat.

As a final note, don't set or lay anything on the paint coat once you've finished, even if it looks totally dry. The solvents will continue to evaporate for some time, and the paint is continuing to cure underneath. Setting a can on the surface before it has cured may just leave you with a nice little indented circle in your beautiful paint coat. Gary Ledford says he knows of a painter who put a mat on the surface and left it there without thinking, only to see the full outline when it was later removed.

Once you finish painting, be sure to thoroughly clean the gun as instructed in the owner's manual, using thinner to clean the canister, as well as the internal components. Never use a piece of wire to try to clean clogged passages.

Finishing the Job

Once you've finished painting the tractor, you may or may not be really finished, depending on the type of paint you used and your own preferences. First of all, you'll need to remove any masking tape and paper after the paint has completely cured. Keep in mind that the layers of paint have no doubt bridged the lip between the paint and the tape, so you need to carefully lift the tape in such a way that it doesn't tear the paint coat. To do this, pull the tape away from the painted area and back on itself rather than

straight up or toward the paint. The idea is to create a sharp angle where the tape contacts the surface. If there is any concern about whether it is going to pull away cleanly, use a sharp razor blade to cut the paint film next to the tape.

As mentioned earlier, some painters like to wet sand the final coat of paint to attain the ultimate smoothness before polishing the surface or applying a clear coat. Others use very fine sandpaper to simply remove the nibs that interfere with a smooth surface. Not all paint coatings will

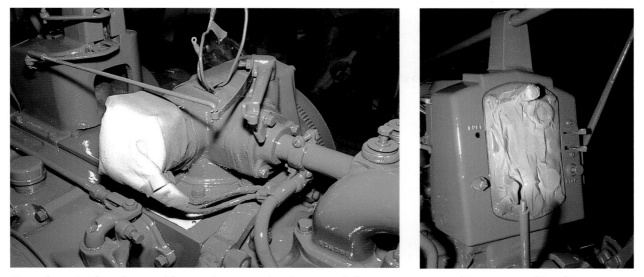

Once the paint has thoroughly cured, you can begin to carefully remove any masking tape and masking paper.

accept wet sanding, so check with your paint supplier ahead of time or at least before doing any wet sanding on the finish. If you do plan to do any wet sanding, use very fine paper with 1,500- to 2,000-grit on a hand-sanding block. Then use just enough light pressure to remove nibs or dust and dirt in the finish.

To be honest, most tractor painters are satisfied with the finished appearance that comes with several coats of enamel that contains a hardener to strengthen the paint and add luster.

Another option, assuming it is permissible with the paint you are using, is to "rub out" any minute imperfections with rubbing compound or polishing compound. More about those products will be covered in Chapter 13 on paint care, but suffice to say polishing compounds include polishing grit to remove blemishes and oxidation of old paint. In this case, the idea is to remove any imperfections and polish the surface to a deeper shine. If you do use a polish, make sure the finish has completely cured and that all the solvents have evaporated. This is one time you can use an electric polisher or buffer, as long as you're using a machine polishing compound.

Finally, if you plan to apply a coat of wax after the polish, it's best to wait at least 90 to 120 days for that step. In the meantime, you're ready to move on to applying the decals and putting your tractor back together.

No matter how good of a job you did painting the tractor, there are often spots, such as nuts and bolts, that have been tightened during reassembly that require touch-up.

CHAPTER 11

COMPONENTS AND ACCESSORIES

It's worth your time to take care of a vintage work light, such as this one on an older John Deere tractor. It's not often you find one like this that still has the original glass.

Although a tractor is somewhat easier to paint than other vehicles (since there's less masking and substantially less sheet metal, which can also be conveniently removed), painting a tractor does pose a few challenges not encountered on a pickup or car. The steering wheel, for example, is usually exposed as part of the unit, and as such, it requires attention to make the whole paint job look acceptable. The same goes for the tractor's lights, which were generally attached to the fenders until a designer decided they would look better inset into the grille sometime late in the 1950s.

So this chapter highlights some of the accessories and components on a tractor that need one last bit of attention when painting.

Lights

Depending upon the age of your tractor, you may not even have to concern yourself with refurbishing the lights. That's because lights didn't become common on farm tractors until the late 1930s, even though they were available on some tractor models as an option much earlier.

Besides broken lenses and deteriorated wiring, the most common problem you're likely to encounter on a tractor light is a rusty, faded, or worn reflector. Most restorers start the renewal process by cleaning the light inside and out, after first disassembling it. One restorer likes to bead blast the light housing to a smooth finish—although he admits that paint stripper can have the same effect.

Now, it's simply a matter of using a galvanizing-effect paint to spray paint the reflector. The outer shell, meanwhile, can be painted at the same time you're painting other tractor components. Should you have any trouble finding a replacement gasket for reassembly, you might also want to use a tip provided by Jeff Gravert, a tractor restorer from Central City, Nebraska. Having learned a number of tricks from his late father, Carroll "Oppy" Gravert, Jeff says a good substitute for the gasket that fits between the lens and the reflector is a strip of caulking that comes in rolls and pulls off like a piece of cord. It also helps hold the lens in place.

Should you need to find a replacement light, keep in mind that swap meets, salvage yards, and dealer parts counters are all good sources. A number

Unless the lights are in good shape and only need to be masked for painting, it's generally best to disassemble the light, paint the rear reflector (unless it's a sealed-beam unit), and repaint the shell before reassembling the unit.

It's pretty obvious that this boat trailer light was never original equipment on a Ford 8N tractor. Obviously, the original owner found it less expensive to "make do."

A set of reproduction lights, in place of the boat trailer light, certainly looks a lot better in terms of a quality restoration.

When he has spare time between restorations, Walter Bieri of Savannah, Missouri, often restores individual parts, like this lineup of headlights, so they're ready when he needs them.

of vendors also offer both reproduction and refurbished lights for sale.

Gauges

Gauges can be a real problem for the restorer trying to obtain an authentic look. Some of the companies that built gauges for the early tractors are no longer in business, while others no longer make gauges that look like the originals. Stewart-Warner (S-W), for instance, makes gauges that work fine for many older tractors. Many of them even look a lot like the original. Unfortunately, most of the current S-W gauges have the S-W logo at the bottom of the gauge face. In contrast, the original usually had no logo at all, or it had the tractor brand name on the gauge face.

Also keep in mind something that applies to so many other things in tractor restoration: It is important you do a little research or talk to other tractor collectors to find out what is authentic. For example, unlike the replacement gauges currently available from John Deere dealers, which feature black faces, the original gauges used on two-cylinder models had white faces and the words "John Deere" on the face. Since John Deere loosened the copyright restrictions, though, the correct gauges are now readily available from several sources.

Still, you may have to make some choices when it comes to gauge replacement. If you're not terribly concerned about originality, you can replace any gauge that is no longer working with an off-the-shelf model, including an S-W gauge or perhaps a new-style brand-name gauge. Or you can contact one of the vendors listed in the back of this book and find a specially built reproduction. Don't overlook the local dealer, though. Thanks to AGCO's emphasis on rebuilding an inventory of vintage parts, AGCO dealers are now able to order a

Whether you install new gauges or existing gauges you've renovated, you can achieve that "like new" look.

number of parts, including certain gauges, for older Oliver, Minneapolis-Moline, Massey-Harris, Massey Ferguson, and Allis-Chalmers tractors.

If a gauge is available from no other source, you can still check the salvage yard. Depending on

Sure, you could find some over-the-counter gauges that would work fine, but there's nothing like reproduction Case gauges to set off a repainted Case tractor.

the reason the tractor ended up there, it may have a gauge that's in better shape than the one on your tractor. If the face-plate is in relatively good shape, it's easy enough to refurbish the rest of the gauge.

To do this, first you'll need to carefully remove the bezel ring that holds the glass in place. On some gauges, you may have to bend up the lip around the edge of the gauge to do so. Now, it's just a matter of cleaning it up, making sure the mechanisms work properly, and repainting it.

Steering Wheel

Unless your tractor has been protected from the elements for most of its life, or you have a very early tractor model with a steel steering wheel, there's a pretty good chance your steering wheel is going to

For a professional look on a hard-rubber-rimmed steering wheel, you might consider sending it to one of several companies that specialize in refurbishing plastic- or wood-rimmed steering wheels.

be severely cracked. Fortunately, you have several options when it comes to fixing it. If you prefer to have the steering wheel professionally repaired, several companies specialize in refurbishing steering wheels. Minn-Kota is one of the most notable; it can take your old wheel and mold new plastic around the steel rim, complete with the original grooves, ribs, or finger ridges.

Should you choose to repair a cracked steering wheel yourself, restorers often choose one of several options. One professional restorer says he uses Fiberstrand body filler to fill all the cracks and crevices. Another uses a body filler such as Evercoat polyester glazing material and follows that with a coat of fast-fill primer. With either product, the steering wheel must be sanded smooth after the material hardens and then painted.

Of course, you can always buy a reproduction or refurbished steering wheel. Just be sure you get the right style for your particular model, assuming authenticity is important to you. Regardless of what route you take, though, the final step on steering wheel restoration will be to carefully mask the restored rubber and repaint the spokes and center hub.

Tires

If the tractor you are painting or restoring has been sitting for some time, it's quite possible that the tires have rotted away after years of sitting in a pasture or, at the very least, have become cracked and weather-checked from months of exposure.

You probably didn't need one more thing to worry about, but unfortunately replacement tires can be rather expensive, especially if you're restoring a large tractor or "wheatland" model. A new set of its 14x34 rear tires can easily set you back at least $700.

If your only goal is to restore and repaint a working tractor, any tires that fit the rim will generally be acceptable. The newer-style tires—with their 23-degree bar, or long-bar/short-bar design—may even offer better traction than the 45-degree lug tires originally found on the tractor.

If, however, your goal is to restore a vintage model to show condition, and you're after accuracy, the challenge is a little greater. Not only did

If you're restoring a work tractor, newer-style tires—with their 23-degree bar—generally offer better traction than the 45-degree lug tires originally found on the tractor. This Model 8N, remanufactured by N-Complete in Wilkinson, Indiana, has been rebuilt from the ground up, including new tires.

the tire companies change their size standards, but they also changed tire styles as more effective patterns were developed. Fortunately, there are several independent sources for the most sought-after sizes and types of tractor tires. They include M. E. Miller, Gempler's, and Wallace W. Wade (see the list of parts sources in Appendix B for addresses and phone numbers).

You also have a few options if you want to recondition a set of tires that are worn or slightly damaged, but still usable. One is to use a can of rubber putty to repair cracks, gouges, weather checking, and other minor problems. Unfortunately, it can't be used to repair a hole. In addition, various companies carry a concentrated black tire paint that can be used to revive the color of old, gray-looking tires. Simply mix it with paint thinner according to the directions on the label and apply it as you would paint.

For those who desire an authentic restoration, vintage tires molded to match the original are available from various sources, including M. E. Miller Tire Company.

CHAPTER 12

DECALS, NAMEPLATES, AND SERIAL NUMBER PLATES

Although the main topic of this book is tractor painting, no paint job would be complete without the decals and nameplates that really set off the finished tractor. So this chapter will provide a few tips on applying and using decals, emblems, and serial number plates.

When it comes to decals, the good news is they have never been easier to apply or easier to find. Fortunately, the interest in antique tractor restoration—coupled with advances in computer-graphics technology—has changed all that. It started when a few collectors commissioned a printer to produce a set of decals that they couldn't locate. Using modern scanning technology, decal manufacturers are now able to produce decals from drawings, literature, operating manuals, or even pencil rubbings.

Due to the research efforts of tractor enthusiasts like Lyle Dumont (left), Lyle Wacker (top), and Gaylen Mohr (right), decals are available for nearly every popular tractor model ever built. Dumont and his wife, Helen, sell decals for Oliver models; Wacker stocks decals for Case and Allis-Chalmers; and the Mohr family manufactures and sells decals for Minneapolis-Moline.

Today's vinyl die-cut decals really make a difference on the appearance of a vintage tractor like this classic Farmall M.

Soon the people who commissioned those companies to print a few decals for their own use found there was a demand for the product and began selling them to other collectors. Thus a whole new business was born.

The other thing that has changed in the industry is the type of decals available. At one time, almost all of the decals on the market were the old water-transfer type, similar to the ones that were once applied on plastic airplane models. After soaking these in water, the backing paper was slipped off and the decal was applied and left to dry.

Even after John Deere started applying decals in 1942, they were the water-transfer type. Unfortunately, water-transfer decals have a limited shelf life, since they tend to crack easily. They also begin to weather and crack very quickly after they have been applied to a tractor. As a result, water-type decals are seldom used today, especially since technology has helped decal suppliers develop better alternatives.

These days, many of the decals sold and used are made by screen printing on to Mylar plastic. With

The majority of the tractor decals used today are made of vinyl die-cut numbers or letters, or a silk-screened piece of Mylar. In both cases, the decal is sandwiched between two layers of protective paper.

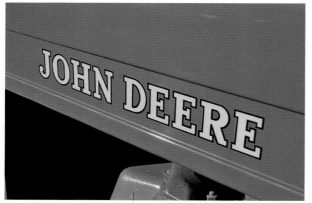

A number of tractor restorers choose to use die-cut vinyl over Mylar whenever possible for obvious reasons. Note, for example, how the clear Mylar is still visible on the decal at top compared to the vinyl die-cut letters above.

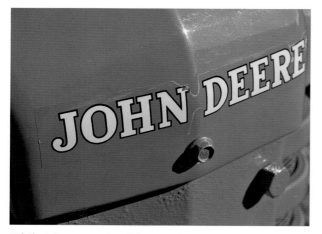

While it's not noticeable at a distance, the clear background on this Mylar decal is already starting to lift and tear, detracting from the overall appearance.

this type of decal, you simply remove the backing paper, which protects the adhesive; carefully press the decal into position; and remove the front layer of paper that protects the letter surface, much like you would apply a bumper sticker.

Equally popular are vinyl-cut decals. Like the Mylar decals, the decal is sandwiched between two layers of protective paper; however, each letter or number is individually cut out of vinyl by either a computer-cut or die-cut method. The paper on the back protects the adhesive, while the paper on the front holds each of the letters in place as they're being applied.

Unfortunately, vinyl-cut decals are often a one-shot deal, without any chance for adjustment, since the letters are all separated from each other.

Researching Decal Originality and Placement

Before you get started with any type of decal, it's important that you have the right tools and the right information. The latter is particularly important. You may think you know where all the decals go, but even experienced restorers get fooled at times. Decal configurations occasionally changed from one year to another, even within the same model. And not all models were equal, either.

For example, the "John Deere" logo decal is centered on the side of the hood on the majority of John Deere tractors built through the early part of the century. According to Travis Jorde, owner of Jorde's Decals and an authority on John Deere decals, Deere moved the "John Deere" decal toward the front of the hood in 1949. An exception was the Model G, which had a radiator shutter bracket that was riveted in place in a location where the rivets interfered with a forward decal position. So the decal on the G remained centered until the shutter bracket was welded in place behind the hood. At that point it, too, received the forward-mounted decal.

Similarly, the words "General Purpose" appeared on the side of the Models A and B along with the words "John Deere" until the middle of the 1935 production year, although they continued to be used on the Model G for a little longer. Meanwhile, the model designation was applied on the rear of the fuel tank until 1935, at which point it was moved to the seat support, where it remained through 1946. The following year, Deere moved it to the hood where it was displayed in a black circle.

Interestingly, Jorde notes, the seat-position decals always included designations for any submodels, such as AN (for single front wheel narrow) or AW (wide front axle). However, after the company introduced the round decal, only the orchard (AO or BO) and wheatland versions (AR and BR) were identified. An A with a single front wheel was just designated as an A.

By the way, the seat-support designation decal on John Deere two-cylinder tractors should always be positioned so that it is readable from the belt pulley side.

Other noteworthy highlights in the decal progression occurred in 1935, when Deere dropped the leaping deer that had previously appeared between the words "John" and "Deere," and 1942, when the company changed the "John Deere" lettering style.

Other brands have their own set of quirks. For example, International Harvester sponsored a tractor repainting program in the 1950s, which effectively changed the decal location on hundreds of Farmall and McCormick tractors. Whether it was to help dealerships make some extra money during the slow months or to improve the economy when tractor sales were slow makes little difference today. With few exceptions, the dealership that did the painting installed new decals that were current at the time of the paint job. That means that a 1942 Farmall that was repainted in 1951 received the 1951 decals. The question you have to ask yourself is, "Do I want it to look like an original 1942 model, or do I want it to look like the model I acquired?"

There are plenty of cases, too, where dealers made modifications to correct a factory problem. If it involved sheetmetal replacement, as was the case with early Farmall M models (to fix a vibration), new decals were provided. Again, these were generally current decals, which changed the tractor

It's important to know the correct decal location before you start this final stage. For example, on early John Deere A and B tractors, the model designation was on the back of the fuel tank.

Unless you took measurements before you stripped off the old paint and decals, or used an accurately restored model as a reference, it can be difficult to position decals in the correct location, especially if they don't run parallel to a seam or the edge of the hood.

from its original appearance. No doubt there were similar situations with other tractor manufacturers and dealers.

Beware of All-Inclusive Kits and Cheap Copies

Experienced tractor restorers insist you also need to be careful when buying a package of decals that includes logos and lettering for more than one tractor model. If there are extra decals in the package, people often feel like they need to use them.

Travis Jorde provides just one example. "There's one decal that comes in a number of sets from John Deere that states, 'Keep valve closed when not running,' he says.

"Well, people naturally think that if it refers to valves it must go somewhere on the engine. As a result, I've seen that decal stuck in all kinds of

The model number decal that fits on the seat bracket of early John Deere two-cylinder tractors always includes the designation for the submodels. It should always be positioned so that it is readable from the belt pulley side.

places. The restorer figures that if it's in the kit, it must go somewhere. The fact is that particular decal refers to the valve on the LP tank and is applied to the side of the tank on LP tractors only."

To help avoid such confusion, many decal suppliers have developed a specific kit for each tractor model. Moreover, the kit includes only the decals that are to be used on that particular model. Of course, that means you need to know at least the year, model number, and engine type for your tractor. In cases where there was a midyear change in decals, you'll also need the serial number if you want to ensure accuracy.

Eugene Mohr, who creates decals for Minneapolis-Moline tractors, relates that there is a difference between the decals used on a propane model and those used on a gas model, even though the model may be the same. So do the research before you start. Look up old sales brochures or owner's manuals, look at old photographs, and talk to club members from collector organizations.

Lyle and Helen Dumont, who sell decals for the majority of Oliver tractor models, insist they hand-assemble all kits so a restorer gets all of the decals he or she needs for a particular model without getting confused by extra decals that don't apply to that unit. While most orders can be filled with the model and year number only, there are a few cases, they say, where it's necessary to also provide a serial number. This is particularly true with the Fleetline Series, which had a decal change during the 1951 model year.

"When we started the business, we had to scrounge original decals from every place you can imagine," says Lyle Dumont, who also sells decals for Hart-Parr, Oliver Hart-Parr, and a few Cockshutt tractors. "The best thing we could hope for was to find an old set of decals at a dealership. That's why I was having to do this in the first place; you couldn't find them. So I'd drag all kinds of sheetmetal parts, including hoods, fenders, and gas tanks, down to the supplier just so they'd have something to copy.

"Once you find something you can copy, you're looking at a setup charge and a die charge," he adds. "Then, you have to get the colors right, so you're

Remember that some decal sets include decals that are not appropriate for your tractor. Use only the ones that are accurate. An example is the decal for LP tractors only that states, "Keep valve closed when not running." Not all models have power steering, either.

paying for a color match, and it just seems to go on and on. Pretty soon, you've got a lot of money involved to where you have to get 500 to 1,000 made in order to make it affordable."

Dumont says his biggest challenge now is ensuring accurate color and dealing with new competitors. "It's still hard to get the true colors down," he says. "You can find two original decals and even those won't be the same color. So we've done a lot of research to get them right.

"Now that we've done all the work and tractor restoration is getting so popular, we're seeing guys take our decals and having them copied and printed overseas where they can get them done cheaper. But you get what you pay for. We've always tried to get superior quality, and that's what most guys still want."

Tools and Supplies

In one respect, applying decals is no different than overhauling the engine—you need the right tools and supplies before you start. This should include a roll of paper towels; a clean, soft cotton towel; a roll of masking tape or drafting tape; and a rubber or plastic squeegee (you can find these in most craft, automotive, and wallpaper supply stores). A sponge may be helpful, as well. Plus, you might want to have a pair of tweezers handy for holding the edge of smaller decals. If you're using wet-application decals, you'll also need a water tray large enough to immerse the decals being applied.

Surface Preparation

Next, make sure the surface has been prepared. First of all, the surface needs to be thoroughly dry. If you are applying Mylar decals to any painted surfaces, you also need to be sure the paint has cured. Travis Jorde notes that depending on the climate in which you live, the paint may require anywhere from a week to a month after the tractor has been painted to fully cure. If a hardener was used in the paint, you may need to wait even longer to make sure the paint isn't going to give off gas bubbles that form under the decal.

Unlike vinyl decals, which have the ability to breathe, Mylar is impermeable to air and gas

Don't forget about the small instructional decals that were a vital part of the original model. However, it's important to know which ones were used and where, since decal kits often apply to several tractor models and include extra decals.

bubbles. So any bubbles that form under the decal after application will stay there. The tractor's paint surface must be smooth and absolutely clean, as well. If there are any pits or surface imperfections, the decal may not adhere properly. Finally, make sure your hands are clean.

You need to make sure the room temperature is within a comfortable range, too. This isn't just for your comfort. The shop should be between around 60 and 90 degrees Fahrenheit to ensure that the decals adhere correctly. Decals don't do well when the temperature or metal is too cold. Worse yet, if you're applying vinyl decals on a hot surface or under a bright sun, they can get too warm and stretch as you're trying to smooth them out and stick them in place.

Decal Application

Now that everything is ready, the first step is to hold the decal in the proper location and mark the edges with a piece of tape. You should be able to see the actual decal outline, even if it does have a protective film on each side. Using a few pieces of tape to mark the bottom edge and a piece of tape on one or both ends will give you a reference point.

At this stage of the game, it's simply a matter of peeling off the backing and applying the numbers or lettering to the tractor. Still, keep in mind some of the tips below. These will make the job easier.

Mylar Decals

If you're using Mylar decals, you would be wise to make sure your hands and tools are clean and wet, as many veteran restorers do. This will help keep the decal from sticking to surfaces it's not supposed to.

Some restorers, like Iowa's Jim Seward, also like to use a spray bottle filled with water and a single drop of soap to spray the metal surface. You should also fill a cake pan or similar-size container with water and another drop of soap. Then you can run the decal through the pan of water before placing it on the metal.

"The only purpose of the soap is to break the surface tension of the water, so you don't need

The first step in decal application is to position the decal in the proper location and tack it in place with pieces of tape.

much," Seward says. "It gives the water a sheeting action, instead of beading up."

Another option used by some restorers, including John Hunter of Hunter-Maple Decals, is to use Windex for the same purpose. Just be sure you use a formula that does not contain ammonia, as it can damage the paint and cause it to fade in sunlight. Also, use the form that comes in a pump-spray bottle. An aerosol can produces too many bubbles, Hunter warns.

It may seem that the water or liquid is used so you can remove the decal or shift it around if you make a mistake. "And you can do that," Seward says. "The main reason you should wet a Mylar decal, though, is so you can more easily squeeze out all the air bubbles."

Remember, Mylar doesn't breathe. If there are any air bubbles under the decal once it dries, they're tough to get out.

Depending upon their position, decals can be hinged at the top or bottom for easier installation.

When applying decals, it's best to have a pan or bottle of water handy to wet the decal and the metal surface, which makes it easier to squeeze out any air bubbles that are trapped under the decal.

Once the decal is in the exact location you want it, use the squeegee to press the decal into place and remove any water and air bubbles from beneath it. Start in the center and work outward. Then use a soft cloth to dry the surface and remove any adhesive left on the surface.

Vinyl Decals

Unlike Mylar decals, vinyl decals can be applied almost immediately after painting, since the material will allow air and solvents to pass through it. Keep in mind, though, that some decal kits will contain both vinyl and Mylar decals. So you will have to treat the latter accordingly.

"Some decals are only available in Mylar, and some come in a choice of vinyl and Mylar," John Hunter says. "We let the customer decide which type they want."

When it comes to vinyl decals, some restorers simply mark the position with a few pieces of tape, peel off the backing, and stick the decals in position using the tape as a guide. There's another method, however, that can save time and reduce the margin of error.

To begin, place the decal in the correct position and "tack" it in place with a few pieces of tape. Once you have ensured it is in the right spot, run a piece of tape across the full length of the top. This piece of tape acts as a hinge for the decal. Next, remove the pieces of tape that acted as a temporary tack, leaving only the top hinge. Now, all you have to do is lift up the decal, pull off the backing, and drop it back down into position.

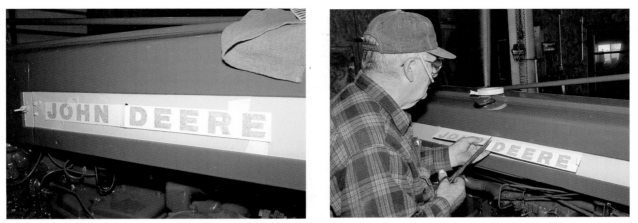

Travis Jorde, owner of Jorde Decals, suggests running a piece of tape across the top of the decal to act as a hinge when placing it. It also helps to cut long decals—such as the John Deere lettering decal on the side of most John Deere two-cylinder tractors—between the words, making the decal more manageable to place.

By lifting the decal on its tape hinge, you can then peel off the paper backing and . . .

Drop the decal directly into position and press it down firmly.

Once the decal has been pressed in place, carefully peel off the protective coating paper.

As a final step, wipe the surface with a soft, clean cloth to press out any air bubbles and dry the surface.

If you're working with a long decal, such as a decal that goes along the side of the hood, you can generally cut it into two pieces, separating it between words or letters, so it's easier to work with. Examples include the long "John Deere" and "International Harvester" decals used on the appropriate models. To finish it off, simply press the decal in place, remove the top protective paper, and smooth everything with a soft, dry cloth.

Seward says another option is to securely tape a long decal at the top and bottom in the middle and pull the paper toward the ends. This allows you to handle long decals one half at a time.

Don't worry if you have a few little bubbles this time. All you have to do is set the tractor out in the sun. The pores in the vinyl will open up and allow the air to permeate through the decal, leaving a smooth surface. As stated earlier, just don't try to apply the vinyl decals in the sun. They may stretch.

Clear Coat or Not?

Although some restorers like to finish off the decals with a shot of clear coat, others say they never put paint or clear coat over any kind of decal. For one thing, you have to know that the decal can take it and that the protectant won't cause it to lift off the surface. Water transfer decals, for one, can't be covered with clear coat.

Travis Jorde says the company that supplies the vinyl for his decals won't warranty the product if it's sprayed with clear coat, and he insists the clear coat manufacturers don't suggest it either. He has applied clear coat over decals himself, however, and hasn't had any problems. So has Jeff McManus, former manager of the Moline Tractor and Plow Company, which restores all the tractors for Deere and Company. McManus says he routinely finishes a tractor by applying the decals and giving all the sheet metal a final layer of clear coat.

The best paint and decal job in the world will lack something if the emblem that adorns the grille on many tractors is not restored or replaced.

They are not cheap, but plenty of sources carry reproduction stainless-steel Farmall emblems and model number emblems, such as those used on the 400 and 450 models.

Some decals do have a tendency to yellow when covered with clear coat, even if the surface is better protected. One body shop owner who paints tractors on occasion says he never puts clear coat over any kind of decal or appliqué, including pin stripes on an automobile, simply because it's a lot easier to replace a decal in the future than it is to restore the paint finish.

Travis Jorde agrees, noting, "If you happen to have problems with a decal, say something gouges a letter, you can replace a single letter. But if you covered the decal with clear coat, that gloss is not going to be on the new letter. Plus, you're going to have a more difficult time getting it off."

In the end, it appears the choice is up to you as the restorer and your willingness to take chances in the interest of appearance.

Emblems and Nameplates

In most cases, a decal is the extent of any adornment or identification you will find on an early-model farm tractor. The exception is the occasional use of an emblem or ornament on the radiator cap. These began appearing on tractors around the same time auto makers started adding chrome and special emblems to cars coming off factory lines. In the case of International Harvester, special emblems first appeared on its tractors in about 1939 with the introduction of the Letter Series.

A new reproduction nameplate on the front grille certainly complements the flawless paint job on this Farmall M restoration.

When Raymond Loewy redesigned Farmall tractors, his assignment included not only the tractors and their controls, but the company logo, as well. His new design for a logo was based on a capital "H" with a small, dotted "I" in the center. It not only included both letters for International Harvester, but viewed straight on, it was designed to suggest the appearance of a row-crop tractor and a driver.

On a number of models, the new logo appeared as an emblem on the front of the hood. On other models, or later versions of the same model, the

Thanks to the growing popularity of tractor restoration, the hood emblems for nearly all of the major brands are available as reproduction parts.

New or reproduction Ford and Ferguson System emblems make all the difference on this Ford 9N restoration.

The NAA Golden Jubilee sported a special cyclops emblem that appeared on 1953 models only. Naturally, the Jubilee emblem is available through restoration parts vendors.

word "Farmall" was spelled out in chrome letters on a distinctive hood emblem.

International Harvester didn't limit its use of emblems and lettering to the grille, however. With the advent of the Number Series in 1954, virtually all numbers and letters were in the form of raised stainless-steel emblems. Whether they appear on a solid red background, as is the case with the 100, 200, and 300, or on a white panel, like that of the 350 and 450, there's nothing as striking as a glossy paint job highlighted with bright, shiny lettering. Again, side emblems are readily available as reproductions and range from around $35 to $50 per emblem.

John Deere, on the other hand, didn't utilize an emblem until 1956 when the company introduced the 20 Series. That's when Deere started using its distinctive green and yellow emblem on the front of the hood.

Of course, being the brainchild of an automotive genius, Ford has used nameplate emblems from the day the 9N tractor was introduced in 1939. In fact, the only things to identify the 9N as a Ford model were its unique style for its time and the two-piece Ford and Ferguson System emblem set on the front of the hood. There was no decal on the side, or anywhere else on the machine.

Unfortunately, most hood emblems are in a position where they can be easily damaged while working with a loader or when the owner "bumps" into something in the back of the machine shed. Because of that, you'll find that many hood emblems have been damaged on vintage tractors. The good news is that the emblems are still readily available, which means it's easier to find a reproduction than to restore the original. It will look a lot better in the end, too.

According to a couple of websites, the Ford/ Ferguson System set, as an example, will run you between $25 and $50, while a Ford Jubilee or 800 medallion will cost you $50 or more. However, as has been mentioned many times before, it's important to know a little something about the history of your tractor. The Ford Jubilee/NAA models built in 1953 and 1954 provide a case in point. Since it marked the 50th anniversary of the Ford Motor Company, only the 1953 Jubilee model used the Jubilee hood emblem that listed the anniversary dates. The 1954 NAA uses a similar but different emblem that has stars around the outside. So it's important you check the serial number and cross-reference it with the catalog listings to make sure you've selected the correct emblem for your model before placing any order.

Hand-Painted Lettering

Depending upon the tractor model you're restoring or painting, you may encounter raised letters on the cast iron or sheet metal that were originally painted. A few examples include the Oliver name that graced the front grille for several years of Oliver tractor production, the John Deere name molded into the axles on several vintage models, and the company name, e.g., Twin City, molded into the radiator casting on a number of early tractor models.

Another very prominent example involves the Ford insignia embossed into the sheetmetal hood, which first appeared on the Model 8N, released in 1948. Not only was the lettering raised, but it was painted red to contrast with the lighter gray hood. In 1950, the Ford script was also embossed into the rear fenders. At the time of manufacture, the letters in both cases were highlighted with a hard paint roller.

Today's Ford tractor restorers have a choice on how best to apply the red coating. Due to the interest in restoration, several companies now offer a painting mask for both the hood and the fenders that can be placed over the script for painting the letters. Some of those same companies, plus several others, also offer a set of die-cut decals.

Some claim the mask is hard to use and requires an experienced hand to make it look good; however, the die-cut decals don't leave much room for error either, since they need to be correctly aligned

A number of early vintage tractors had the brand name or other identification cast into a radiator or axle housing, which calls for hand painting the letters after the rest of the tractor has been painted and allowed to cure.

Beginning with the Model 8N, Ford began embossing the company name into the hood. The raised letters, which were later added to the fenders, too, were then painted red. Today's tractor painter has several options. Some companies make decals to fit on top of the raised letters. Others make a template to fit over the letters while spray painting the raised area. Or you can have a sign painter or a talented friend paint the letters.

from the start to lie as they should across the tops of the letters.

Most experienced Ford show tractor restorers feel the best way to apply the red-painted highlight to the raised hood and fender script is to get a professional sign painter to hand-letter it with an artist's brush. A good sign painter with a steady hand can easily do the raised lettering in just a few minutes and make it look far better than the decal or a stencil paint job. The result, they insist, is usually well worth the cost.

The same could be said for the raised letters on the axle housing, radiator castings, etc. In most of these cases, there isn't a mask or decal available—leaving you with the option of painting it yourself or taking the sign painter route.

Serial Number Plates

For most vintage tractor restorers, restoration of the serial number plate is not only the last step in the project, but a source of pride. Having a tractor with a low serial number is kind of like acquiring a limited-edition painting with a low number. Consequently, tractor collectors don't take this step lightly.

If you're working with an older-model tractor, you may be lucky enough to have a brass serial number plate. If so, a good polishing with brass cleaner will suffice.

Most of the serial number plates on later-model tractors were made of aluminum, however. Of course, like everything, there are exceptions. Ford, for instance, stamped most of its tractor serial numbers into the engine block or transmission case. The problem for collectors is that if the engine was replaced at some time in the past, they have a hard time determining the true age of the tractor without looking for other clues.

Still, you can make the numbers stand out in a couple of ways. If it's stamped into the block or transmission, carefully clean the grooves and make sure the paint isn't applied too heavily to the area. If the numbers are stamped into an aluminum or steel plate, you may just want to clean and polish the plate with steel wool or a quality cleaner.

In cases where the serial number is raised, some restorers have even been known to paint the entire

To finish off your restoration, be sure to clean and polish the serial number plate. Some restorers like to paint aluminum plates with black paint and then lightly sand the paint off the raised lettering. Brass plates, however, are best finished with a good brass cleaner and polish.

plate with black paint. Then, once it has dried, they lightly sand the raised areas with very fine-grit sandpaper so the letters and numbers stand out in stark contrast to the black background.

In some situations, the serial number plate isn't the only plate used on the tractor. Again using Ford tractors as an example, the 9N, 2N, and 8N models display a patent data plate that lists all the patents filed by Ford for the respective models. On the 9N and 2N, the plate is located on the dash panel, and on 8N models, it is on the side of the battery box. Hopefully, if you're restoring one of these models, you removed it before stripping paint and repainting the box or dash panel. Fortunately, in this case, reproductions are available.

Even if the tractor doesn't have a separate serial number plate, and the number is simply stamped into the engine block, some restorers like to set off the serial number, especially if it's on a unique model, such as the 1,310th Model 9N built in 1939.

CHAPTER 13

PAINT CARE

Whether you're trying to preserve a finish that has been previously applied to the tractor, or simply want to protect the paint coat you applied a few chapters earlier, it's important to keep the finish clean. Of course, one of the best ways to do that is with soap and water. But what kind of soap? If you go to the local auto parts store, you'll find dozens of different automotive products for cleaning and caring for painted surfaces. Even more cleaners and soaps can be found at the discount store and grocery store.

So first, I'll cover what not to use. This includes all non-automotive-type wash soaps, including dishwashing detergents and other sudsing cleaners. Most of these are formulated to remove grease and wax, which are not too chemically different from automotive wax. You need to realize, too, that it's not the amount of suds that matters, but how the detergent cleans. You want something that is strong enough to clean off all of the dirt, bugs, tar, and grime, yet not strip the important stuff (like waxes and sealers) from your paint—which is what automotive washing agents are formulated to do.

Next, try to find an area in the shade where you can wash your tractor. If at all possible, avoid washing it in direct sunlight, and never wash a tractor when the sheet metal is hot to the touch. If it is unusually hot or you're forced to wash

If possible, find a shady area for washing your tractor or wait for a cloudy day so you avoid washing the tractor when the sheet metal is hot. Then start by rinsing off all loose dirt with a strong stream of water.

Select a soap product designed for automotive finishes. Dishwashing soaps and household cleaners can strip off protective waxes and sealers. Then gather a bucket and sponge or wash mitt for hand washing.

Not only do the long, soft fibers of a natural sponge or a sheepskin wash mitt hold more suds and water, but the deep nap provides a place for dirt and debris to accumulate so it won't scratch the paint surface before it's rinsed off.

Don't push the mitt too deep into the bucket when rinsing it off. You certainly don't want to pick up dirt that has already been washed off the tractor and allowed to settle to the bottom of the bucket. That's why you also want to have plenty of water and suds in the bucket before you start.

the tractor in the sun, be sure to keep it wet and cool with regular spraying of water.

Start by hosing down the engine, frame, and sheet metal with a thick, strong stream of water. Try to avoid using a narrow jet of water, especially on the sheet metal. Instead, concentrate on loosening dirt and unwanted buildup. If you're going to be using a bucket of water mixed with an automotive-type wash, have it ready before you move on to wetting down the tractor. You shouldn't let any water dry on the paint while filling up the bucket.

According to the experts at Autogeek.net, an online car care source for auto detailing supplies, it's important to also use the right tools when washing a vehicle. In fact, they insist that "most of the swirl marks that disfigure a paint coat are likely caused by poor washing technique."

Consequently, they advise using a clean sheepskin wash mitt or a large-pore sponge for washing any painted sheetmetal surfaces. The idea is that the deep nap will provide a place for dirt and debris to accumulate. The long, soft fibers of a natural sponge, for example, will not scratch the paint, yet they will essentially pull contamination into the sponge's openings, away from the paint. In contrast, a towel or other short-nap cloth can collect dirt and debris close to the surface where it can scratch the finish at the same time you're trying to wash it.

Whether you're using a sponge or mitt, be sure to rinse it often with the hose and soak it periodically in the bucket as you clean. Also, start from the top down when washing the hood, grille, or fenders. It doesn't make sense to drain dirty water over an area you've already covered. Finally, be careful about pushing the sponge or mitt too far into the soap bucket. The heavier dirt and grime are going to accumulate at the bottom, so swishing the sponge around too close to the bottom only offers the potential to pick the

Use a soft-fiber brush to work the dirt loose on the engine, frame, and cast components around the tractor.

After you've finished hand washing, thoroughly rinse the tractor before the soapy water has a chance to dry on the surface. If it's a large tractor, you might want to break the job up into sections.

After washing and rinsing, the tractor should be thoroughly dried with a soft towel. Some tractor enthusiasts prefer deep-pile bath towels, while others prefer the new microfiber towels. It's best not to use a chamois, though, unless the tractor already has a good coat of wax.

dirt and grit back up again. With that in mind, it should go without saying that if you drop a mitt, sponge, or rag that you're using as a wash material on the ground, it should be replaced or thoroughly cleaned before reuse. Remember, even the smallest particles left behind can scratch the paint.

Obviously, a sheepskin mitt isn't going to work on the frame or engine. Here, you might want to resort to a synthetic or animal-hair brush that's effective for working dirt from cracks. Again, rinse the cleaning device with the hose frequently to remove accumulated dirt and grime.

As a final note, don't let water dry on any surface as you wash, particularly sheet metal. Instead, spray water onto the tractor after you've covered each major component, such as the hood, fenders, grille, or engine.

Drying the Finish

The best thing for drying the sheetmetal finish on a car, pickup, or tractor is a soft natural or synthetic chamois, right? Actually, most automotive care professionals say that is the wrong thing to use. The chamois material—especially a natural chamois—develops friction when pulled across the paint that is sometimes sufficient to distort and/or strip wax from the paint surface. In addition, experts insist that the short nap of a chamois increases the chance that any particles that weren't previously washed off the surface will be picked up and rubbed directly into the paint, causing scratches or swirl marks. The same principle would apply to the use of a squeegee to remove excess water.

The better alternative is to use soft cotton towels with plenty of "pile" to cushion dirt and debris picked up while drying. Microfiber towels are also recommended by most cleaning product manufacturers. Pound for pound, they hold more water than cotton towels, and they won't scratch the paint.

Keep in mind that you may not be able to dry the entire tractor fast enough to avoid seeing a few water spots. Fortunately, a quick squirt of detailing spray, such as Mothers, Showtime, Instant Detailer, or Meguiars NXT Generation Speed Detailer, followed by a towel rub, will remove all but severe water spotting. In the case of the latter, you may need to follow up with a cleaner or polish.

Most importantly, don't use the drying towel to remove dirt that you missed while washing, as you risk scratching the paint. Instead, rewash the surface or use a product designed to dissolve the material before wiping it off with a clean towel.

Cleaners and Polish

Now that the tractor has been thoroughly washed, it's time to evaluate the paint surface and the possible need for a cleaner, polish, and/or wax. In general, a good coat of wax should provide protection for three to four months; however, that is greatly dependent on your geographic location, how the tractor is stored, and how much it is exposed to the elements.

It's important to note, too, that dull-looking paint can be attributed to both "above surface defects" and "below surface defects." The former, which include everything from bird droppings to tar and tree sap, can often be removed with a good wash job or at the very least a cleaner or polish. However, below surface defects, which include scratches, oxidation, and acid rain etching, require more serious attention.

Start with a mild abrasive designed to gently remove paint defects (with the emphasis on mild). In fact, automotive care professionals recommend you start with the least abrasive product, like Meguiars Body Scrub or Mothers Pre-Wax Cleaner, and test it on the worst defect to see if it eliminates the problem. If not, move on to something more abrasive, reserving the least abrasive product for the areas with the least problems.

Although a rotary buffer can be used to remove the cleaner, it's generally best to do the whole job by

Depending on the condition of the paint coat on the sheet metal, you can go straight to wax or use a cleaner and/or polish to prepare the finish for wax. This three-step system from Meguiar's is formulated to handle cleaning, polishing, and waxing. At the very least, most paint professionals recommend a protective coat of carnauba wax.

hand to avoid the possibility of "burning" the paint from too much friction. Using a foam applicator pad, spread the product over a limited area using small, circular, overlapping strokes. Remember to let the product do the work rather than trying to do it with heavy pressure; otherwise, you risk the chance of grinding debris back into the paint.

Finally, use a soft terrycloth towel folded into fourths to remove the cleaner. Use one side to carefully remove the material; then flip it over to remove any additional residue. Keep changing the wiping surface so you don't begin wiping the surface with a portion of the cloth that is so dirty that it acts like an abrasive.

If you're using a polish instead of a cleaner, you should follow the same basic procedure as above. Just be careful when working around edges and sharp curves where the paint is often thinner than on flat surfaces.

Sealing and Waxing

Based on the shine you get from polishing the sheet metal, you may think you're finished at this point. Unfortunately, that shine won't last long unless you do something to protect it. In most cases, that protection comes from a coat of wax, silicone, or polymer. Some people even use more than one

Although the safest bet is to hand-buff the waxed or polished surface, you can use an electric buffer if you're sure there is no debris or dirt left on the surface and the buffer goes slow enough that it doesn't create excessive friction and overheat the waxed surface.

product, applying a polymer sealant and allowing it to dry before moving onto the wax.

If you choose to use a polymer, which is often referred to as a resin glaze or polyresin protectant, carefully follow the directions on the label. You'll even find that some of the new polymer sealants claim they're formulated to provide a lasting shine that rivals that of the best-quality wax, which means you don't have to go any further. For the best of both worlds, though, you can still use both.

With or without the polymer sealant, it's now time to move on to the wax. Unfortunately, the number of choices at your local automotive store may leave you genuinely confused. The first step is to avoid the cleaner/wax and polish/wax combinations. These contain a mild abrasive cleaner or chemical cleaner, which shouldn't be necessary, as they're designed to do in one step what you did with the cleaner and/or polishing compound. You should especially avoid them if you've used a polymer sealant, as they will only scratch the coating you've just applied.

You'll also find a variety of synthetic waxes that are often silicone-based. They have the potential to do a good job, but they can actually leave a dull appearance if you put too much on. The other thing you need to know is that they can impair your ability to do any touchup or spot painting in the near future, since new paint will not stick to any surface that contains even a trace of silicone. Silicone does, however, have the ability to penetrate all the paint layers, including the primer, proving a somewhat longer interval between rewaxing.

Most automotive care specialists, therefore, agree that the best option for a deep, lasting shine is a good-quality carnauba wax, even though it is harder to put on, harder to polish, and requires a lot more work. The good news is the hood and fenders on a tractor involve much less area than the typical automobile.

Carnauba wax is derived from the leaves of the carnauba palm, a plant native to northeastern Brazil. As the hardest wax known to man, it is extremely durable. Ironically, this leads some people to request or recommend 100 percent carnauba wax, which, technically, doesn't exist. Even the so-called 100-percent pure carnauba waxes contain a blend of other products. Still, you'll want to look for a product that lists itself as pure carnauba wax, such as Mothers California Gold Pure Carnauba Wax or Meguiars Gold Class Wax. Most are available as both a liquid or a paste.

Now comes the work. Simply apply the wax sparingly with a damp cloth or applicator using a straight-line motion. Work a small section at a time, moving the cloth the length of whatever panel you're working on. Then let it dry for five minutes or more before wiping it with a soft towel and buffing it out.

Going to such detail may take a lot more elbow grease than simply running your tractor through the local car wash, but you can be assured of one thing: Your prized restoration will certainly get a lot more looks at the next parade or tractor show.

Protecting the Finish During Storage and Travel

One of the best ways to protect the finish on a show tractor, or perhaps even a work tractor that you want to protect during the off-season, is to cover it with a tractor cover or tarp. Even if the tractor has been waxed and is stored inside a shed, it's often a good idea to use a cover, if for no other reason than to protect the finish from insect deposits, bird droppings,

Apply the polish and/or wax using a damp cloth or applicator to cover a small section at a time. It's generally best to wait three to four months before waxing a tractor for the first time after it has been painted.

The finished result is a deep shine that not only attracts attention, but will help repel dust when the tractor joins the others in the storage shed.

Let the wax film dry for five minutes or so before wiping it off with a soft towel and buffing it out.

Jerry Schmutzler, a classic tractor enthusiast from St. Joseph, Missouri, likes to use a microfiber mitt and a towel to keep the sheet metal clean and shiny between tractor shows.

etc. After all, very few tractor restorers have the ability to store their collection in a sealed garage.

In most cases, you can go one of two routes. You can purchase a tractor cover that is designed and shaped especially for a tractor, or you can simply drape it with a canvas or plastic tarp that has been weighted or tied down on the sides and/or corners.

One word of caution, though. Be very careful about what type of cover you use if you leave it on while hauling a tractor to a show or parade. It doesn't take a lot of miles or much time for a plastic or rough tarp to cause damage to the paint coating, particularly if it is loose enough to whip around in the wind. The movement of the material back and forth across the paint as the tractor travels down the road on a trailer or the back of the truck can do as much damage as sandpaper.

Consequently, unless you can find a soft cover that promises to be abrasion-free, you're generally better off leaving the tractor uncovered and cleaning off any mud, bug residue, and water spots once you arrive at your destination.

TROUBLESHOOTING

Hopefully, you've made it to this point, having completed the paint job, without any problems. In case you did run into some, though—or you encounter any later—the most common problems that plague a painter are listed in the following outline (which is strictly alphabetical and not in any order of most common occurrence).

Although there are several references to base-coat/clear-coat finishes and metallic finishes, which won't be applicable to most painters, they have been left in, since some readers may choose to use these types of finishes. This is particularly the case with those who restore show tractors and/or customized tractor pulling tractors.

These tips come courtesy of the Martin-Senour Paint Company.

AIR ENTRAPMENT

Small craterlike openings in or on the paint film.

CAUSE

Trapped or buried air pockets in the wet paint film that rise to the surface and "burst," causing small craters. Lack of atomization is the cause of air entrapment and may be due to one or more of the following:
- Spray gun travel too slow.
- Spray gun distance too close.
- Air pressure too low.
- Improper spray gun setup.

REPAIR

- Sand with 1,200 or finer grit sandpaper, then compound and polish to restore gloss.
- Or sand smooth and refinish.

PREVENTION

- Maintain correct spray gun speed.
- Maintain correct spray gun distance.
- Use the recommended air pressure.
- Use the correct air cap/nozzle/needle recommended for clear coats.

Note: Some cases of air entrapment may have an appearance very similar to solvent pop or dust contamination; however, air entrapment normally occurs when the film is still wet and can be removed with compounding procedures. On the other hand, solvent pop will appear after the film is "skinned over" and, when sanded, will have pinholes. Dust contamination will appear while the film is drying, but still "tacky." These craters, under close examination, will have a speck of dirt in the center of the crater.

BLEEDING

(Discoloration)
A red or yellow discoloration in the top-coat color.

CAUSE

Solvent in the new top coat dissolves soluble dyes or pigments in the original finish, allowing them to seep into and discolor the new top coat.

REPAIR

- Allow color to cure. Isolate with two-component undercoat(s) and refinish.
- Or remove original paint film and refinish.

PREVENTION

Isolate suspected bleeding finish by applying a two-component surfacer and/or sealer. Allow to cure following product recommendations; then apply desired top coat.

BLISTERING

(Pimples, Bubbles, Bumps)
Swelled areas appearing as pimples or bubbles in the top-coat film, often months after application.

CAUSE

- Moisture trapped beneath the paint film due to:
(1) Improper dry time after wet sanding.
(2) Contaminated air lines.
(3) Spraying in extreme high humidity conditions.

- Using a poor grade and/or too fast of an evaporating thinner/reducer for spray conditions.
- Trapped solvents from applying wet heavy coats with insufficient flash time between coats.
- Improper dry time of undercoats before top coating.
- Painting over grease, oil, or rust.

REPAIR
- Remove affected area and refinish.
- Extreme cases must be stripped to bare substrate before refinishing.

PREVENTION
- If wet sanding is preferred, allow sufficient time for moisture to evaporate. Avoid wet sanding lacquer-type primer surfacer when possible. Drain moisture from compressor and air lines regularly. Allow additional flash time between coats and/or add retarder when spraying in humid conditions, or spray at times of low humidity when possible.
- Select proper thinner/reducer for spray conditions.
- Apply materials according to product recommendations, allowing sufficient flash time between coats.
- Allow undercoats to thoroughly dry/cure before top coating.
- Clean and prep substrate using recommended products and procedures.

BLUSHING
(Milkiness)
A milky gray cloud appears on the surface of the paint film immediately or shortly after application.

CAUSE
When spraying during humid conditions, air from the spray gun and solvent evaporation lowers the substrate temperature below the dew point, causing moisture in the air to condense in or on the paint film. The condition is aggravated when unbalanced thinner/reducer is used or the thinner/reducer is too fast drying.

REPAIR
- Should blushing occur during application, you should apply heat to the affected area or add retarder and apply additional coats.
- If the finish has dried, minor blushing may be corrected by compounding or polishing; however, severe blushing will require sanding and refinishing.

PREVENTION
- Always use good-quality solvent and thin/reduce material according to label directions.
- Select proper thinner/reducer for spray conditions.
- Add the recommended amount of retarder when spraying in humid conditions.
- Apply heat after application to evaporate moisture.

CHALKING
(Fading, Oxidation, Weathering)
A chalky white appearance on the surface of the paint film.

CAUSE
Pigment is no longer held and protected by resin, resulting in a powderlike surface and lack of gloss due to:
- Natural weathering of the paint film.
- Improper application of paint material.
- Using generic thinner/reducer and/or hardener in the paint material.
- Excessive use of mist/fog coats when applying single-stage finishes.

REPAIR
- Use compound to remove oxidation and polish to restore gloss.
- Or sand the area to remove "weathered" paint film and refinish.

PREVENTION
- Weekly washing and occasional polishing or waxing will remove oxidation from the finish.
- Thoroughly stir, shake, or agitate all paint materials.
- Use the recommended thinner/reducer, hardener, and measure accurately.
- When spraying single-stage metallic finishes, apply mist/fog coats panel by panel while finish is still wet.

CHEMICAL STAINING/ETCHING
(Spotting, Acid Rain, Discoloration)
Irregular-shaped pitting, etching, or discoloration on the paint film.

CAUSE
A chemical change occurs when harmful environmental contaminants, such as acid rain, tree sap, bird droppings, or road tar remain on the surface for an extended period of time.

REPAIR

- Wash the component or panel with soap and hot water; then rinse and dry.
- Clean with appropriate surface cleaner.
- Wash with baking soda solution and rinse thoroughly. (Use one tablespoon baking soda per one quart water.)
- Compound damaged surface and polish to restore gloss.
- If polishing does not remove the damage, wet sand with 1,500- to 2,000-grit sandpaper. Then compound and polish to restore gloss.
- If refinishing is necessary, sand to remove damaged area with appropriate grit sandpaper, wash with a baking soda solution, then refinish. In severe cases, the finish must be removed to bare metal.

PREVENTION

- Remove harmful water-soluble contaminants by regularly washing with detergent and clear water.
- Polish or wax periodically.
- Refinish with an acrylic urethane base-coat/clear-coat system to provide the maximum protection.
- When sanding and buffing a base-coat/clear-coat finish, a minimum film thickness of the clear coat (2 mils) is required to maintain adequate ultraviolet protection. If correcting the damage will result in removing more than 0.5 mils, refinishing is recommended.

CHIPPING

(Nicks, Stone Pecks, Chips, Bruises)
Small areas of damage to the paint film, leaving a nick, notch, or void in the finish.

CAUSE

Loss of adhesion of the paint film to the substrate caused by an impact from stones or other hard objects.

REPAIR

Sand and featheredge damaged areas to remove chips; then refinish.

PREVENTION

- Use premium two-component undercoat and top-coat system.
- Use a flex agent in undercoat and/or top-coat system in areas that are prone to chipping.

COLOR MISMATCH

(Off Shade, Off Color)
The original finish and repair exhibit a noticeable difference in color when viewed under the same lighting conditions.

CAUSE

- Original finish has drifted from manufacturer's standard.
- Old finish weathered and oxidized.
- Color over- or underreduced.
- Improper spray procedures.
- Color not properly stirred or shaken.
- Improper spray gun setup.
- Inaccurate mixing of the color formula.
- "Panel" painting instead of blending.
- Evaluating color under a light source other than color-corrected lighting or natural light.
- Adjusting a color before it has been sprayed, or adjusting a base coat before applying clear coat.

REPAIR

- If color is close enough to blend: prepare adjacent panel(s) for blending, then blend color into adjacent panels.
- If color must be tinted: (1) tint the color for a blendable match, (2) prepare adjacent panel(s) for blending, then (3) respray the repair, blending into the adjacent panel(s).

PREVENTION

- Check alternate color selector for variances. Choose the alternate that provides a blendable match.
- All color must be viewed under equal gloss; compound or polish the area to be matched.
- Thin/reduce according to label directions.
- Follow label directions for proper application of color coat.
- Stir or shake materials thoroughly to be sure all pigments and metallics are mixed properly and the solution is in suspension.
- Refer to product label or data sheet for spray gun, fluid nozzle, and air cap recommendations.
- Recheck color code, formula number, or formula weights before mixing colors.
- Spray a test panel prior to application to determine if blending or tinting is necessary.

- Always use natural daylight or color-corrected lights to make color-matching decisions.
- All color must be sprayed out for an accurate evaluation. Base coats must have clear coat applied. Check color from all angles—face (90 degrees) and side tone (20 to 60 degrees).

CRACKING
(Checking, Crazing, Splitting, Alligatoring, Crowsfeet)
Cracks or lines of various lengths and widths in the top-coat finish, often resembling the cracking of dried mud.

CAUSE
- Excessive film thickness of the undercoat and/or top coat.
- Refinishing over a previously crazed/cracked surface.
- Insufficient flash time between coats and/or force drying undercoats using air from the spray gun.
- Mixing incorrectly or using too much hardener.
- Not thoroughly stirring or agitating paint ingredients.
- Breakdown of finish due to prolonged exposure to sunlight, moisture, and extreme temperature changes.
- Using generic reducers and/or hardeners.

REPAIR
Remove all cracked paint film and refinish.

PREVENTION
- Apply all materials following label direction.
- Completely remove crazed/cracked finishes before refinishing.
- Do not force-dry undercoats by fanning with spray gun air.
- Mix ingredients thoroughly using the recommended additives. Add each component in proper sequence following the recommended mixing ratio.
- Stir or agitate materials thoroughly before use to ensure all ingredients are in solution.
- Use premium two-component undercoat and top-coat system to provide maximum gloss and durability.
- Use the recommended thinner/reducer and hardener, and then measure accurately.

DUST CONTAMINATION
(Dirt in Finish)
Foreign particles embedded in paint film.

CAUSE
- Inadequate cleaning of the surface to be painted.
- Dirty spraying environment.
- Inadequate air filtration or unfiltered air entering the booth.
- Dirty or unsuitable work clothes that contain dust, lint, or fibers.
- Particles from deteriorated air supply lines.
- Poor-grade masking paper.
- Dirty spray gun.
- Removing the vehicle from the spray booth before the finish is "dust-free."

REPAIR
- Sand with 1,200 or finer grit sandpaper. Then compound and polish to restore gloss.
- Or sand smooth and refinish.

PREVENTION
- Thoroughly blow off all parts to be painted and clean all surrounding areas. Wipe the surface to be painted, along with any masking paper, with the tack rag.
- Maintain a clean working area.
- Wear a lint-free paint suit during the spray application.
- Use quality masking materials. "Wicks" found on newspaper can break away and blow into the wet paint.
- Repair or replace defective air compressor lines and/or hoses.
- Properly clean and maintain spray equipment.
- Tractor or components should be kept in a clean environment until finish is "dust-free."

Note: Fine dust particles that fall on a tacky surface can be encapsulated by the finish, creating an appearance almost identical to solvent pop. This "solvent pop" appearance usually occurs on vehicles that are removed from the booth in a tacky condition and placed in another location to dry. Fine dust contamination can be removed by sanding and polishing; however, if the condition is solvent pop, the finish will contain pinholes or small craters after sanding.

EDGE MAPPING

(Edge Ringing, Featheredge Lifting)

Raised or lifted edges in the wet or dry paint film that outline sand-throughs or featheredges.

CAUSE

Solvent from the new top coat penetrates a solvent-sensitive substrate, causing a lifting or wrinkling that outlines the featheredge.

REPAIR

- Sand smooth or remove the affected area. Final sand with 400 or finer grit sandpaper.
- Isolate affected area with a two-component primer surfacer and refinish.
- Or apply waterborne primer surfacer, sand smooth, and refinish.
- Or apply acrylic lacquer primer surfacer thinned with nonpenetrating thinner, sand smooth, and refinish.

PREVENTION

- Check questionable finishes by rubbing a small, inconspicuous area with a shop towel saturated with lacquer thinner. Finishes susceptible to lifting will soften, wrinkle, or shrivel as lacquer thinner is applied.
- Use acrylic urethane primer surfacer, waterborne primer surfacer, or an acrylic lacquer primer surfacer thinned with nonpenetrating thinner over sensitive substrates.
- Use 400 or finer grit sandpaper when featheredging.
- Avoid sanding through insoluble top-coat color or clear coat, exposing solvent-sensitive or solvent-soluble finishes.

FISHEYES

(Silicone Contamination, Cratering)

Small, circular, craterlike openings that appear during or shortly after the spray application.

CAUSE

- Spraying over surfaces contaminated with oil, wax, silicone, or grease.
- Use of thinner/reducer in place of a solvent cleaner.
- Spraying over previously repaired areas containing "fisheye eliminator" additive.

REPAIR

- Remove wet paint film with solvent, clean, and refinish.
- Add the recommended fisheye eliminator and respray the affected area.
- If fisheyes appear in a base coat, allow the color to flash; then spray a mist coat over affected area. Do not use fisheye eliminator in undercoats or base-coat color.
- If the paint has dried, sand to a smooth finish below the fisheye cratering and refinish.

PREVENTION

- Thoroughly clean the surface to be painted with detergent and hot water, followed by the recommended solvent cleaner. Wipe dry with clean rags.
- Use fisheye eliminator that is specifically recommended for the top coat.
- Install an air-filtering system that removes and prevents oil and moisture contamination.
- Maintain air supply by draining, cleaning, and changing filter(s) on a routine basis.

LIFTING

(Wrinkling, Raising, Alligatoring, Shriveling, Swelling)

The existing paint film shrivels, wrinkles, or swells during new finish application or drying.

CAUSE

Solvents in a newly applied product attack the previous finish, causing wrinkling, raising, or puckering of the paint film due to:

- Recoating enamels or urethanes that are not fully cured.
- Exceeding maximum flash or recoat times during application.
- Recoating a base-coat/clear-coat finish, where existing clear coat has insufficient film build.

REPAIR

Remove lifted areas and refinish.

PREVENTION

Check questionable finishes by rubbing a small, inconspicuous area with a shop towel saturated with lacquer thinner. Finishes susceptible to lifting will soften, swell, or shrivel as lacquer thinner is applied. If any of these reactions occur, the following recommendations should be considered.

- Do not exceed a product's maximum recoat time during or after application.
- Allow enamels or urethanes to thoroughly cure before recoating or attempting a repair.
- Avoid applying undercoats or top coats excessively wet.
- Avoid the use of lacquer products over an air-dried enamel finish.
- When insoluble material (enamel/urethane) has been applied over a soluble material (lacquer):
(1) Avoid sanding through and exposing areas of the soluble material.
(2) Apply two-component primer surfacer and/or sealer as a barrier between the new and the old finish. When applying two-component undercoats over soluble finishes, the complete panel must be coated.
- Use waterborne undercoats to repair extremely sensitive finishes.

LOSS OF GLOSS

(Hazing, Dulling, Dieback, Matting, Weathering)
A dulling of the gloss as the film dries or ages.

CAUSE

- Top coat applied in heavy, wet coats.
- Inadequate flash time between coats.
- Insufficient film thickness of top-coat color or clear coat.
- Insufficient drying/curling of undercoats before applying top coats.
- Using a poor grade and/or too fast evaporating thinner/reducer for spray conditions.
- Improper cleaning of the substrate.
- Insufficient air movement during and after application.
- Spraying over a deteriorated or solvent-sensitive substrate finish without proper priming or sealing procedures.
- Natural weathering of the finish.

REPAIR

- Allow finish to cure thoroughly, compound, or polish to restore gloss.
- Or sand and refinish.

PREVENTION

- Apply the top coat according to product label directions, using the recommended gun setup and air pressure.
- Allow all coatings sufficient flash between coats.
- Apply sufficient number of coats to achieve recommended proper film thickness.

- Allow undercoats to thoroughly dry/cure before top coating.
- Select recommended thinner/reducer based on temperature, humidity, air movement, and size of repair.
- Clean substrate thoroughly before and after sanding.
- For air dry situations: (1) allow exhaust fan to run 40 minutes or longer after spraying; (2) open booth doors after finish is dust-free; and (3) maintain a shop temperature of 60 degrees Fahrenheit or above, especially when drying overnight.
- For maximum holdout, use a premium two-component undercoat system.
- Properly wash and care for the finish on a regular basis.
- Using a premium top-coat color or clear-coat system will provide maximum gloss and durability.

MOTTLING

(Streaking, Tiger/Zebra Stripes, Floating, Flooding)
A streaked, spotty, or striped appearance in a metallic color.

CAUSE

- An uneven distribution of metallic flake caused by:
(1) Using a spray gun that gives an unbalanced spray pattern.
(2) Improper application technique, such as tilting the spray gun during application, causing the spray pattern to become heavy at the top or bottom.
(3) Holding the gun too close to the surface (flooding).
(4) Uneven spray pattern overlap.
(5) Omitting/improper use of mist coats.
- Too much thinner/reducer. Color overthinned/reduced.
- Applying clear coat to a base coat that has not thoroughly flashed/dried.
- Improper application of base coat (e.g., failure to apply or an improper use of a low-pressure mist coat or wet base-coat application).

REPAIR

- To uniform single-stage metallic finishes, apply a higher-pressure mist coat, panel by panel, while previous coat is still wet.
- Or allow base-coat color to flash; then apply a low-pressure mist coat.
- Finishes that have dried must be sanded and refinished.

Caution: Large areas of base coat must have clear coat applied before sanding, but small nibs or lint may be removed from a base coat by wet sanding, concentrating only on the defect. Apply additional base coat to the sanded area before clear coating.

PREVENTION

- Use recommended spray gun, including fluid tip and air cap, for the material being sprayed. Always adjust the gun for best atomization and balanced spray pattern before paint application.
- Use the correct ratio of thinner/reducer.
- Allow base coat proper flash/dry time before clear coating.
- Follow base coat application procedures.

ORANGE PEEL

(Poor Flow, Texture)

Paint film having an uneven texture that resembles the skin of an orange.

CAUSE

- Underreduction and/or air pressure too low.
- Thinner/reducer evaporates too fast for spray conditions.
- Excessive film thickness or piling on of heavy wet coats.
- Improper spray gun setup.
- Improper painting technique.

REPAIR

- Compound or polish to reduce surface texture.
- Or sand smooth with 1,200 or finer grit sandpaper, compound, and polish to restore gloss.
- Or sand smooth and refinish.

PREVENTION

- Use proper reduction ratio and spray at recommended air pressure.
- Select recommended thinner/reducer based on temperature, humidity, air movement, and size of repair.
- Avoid heavy coats and excessive film thickness.
- Use recommended spray gun, fluid tip, and air cap for the material being sprayed. Always adjust the gun for best atomization and balanced spray pattern before paint application.
- During paint application, hold the gun perpendicular and parallel to the surface. Adjust speed of pass, pattern overlap, and distance from the panel to achieve the desired appearance.

PEELING

(Flaking, Delamination)

A loss of adhesion or separation of the paint film from the substrate.

CAUSE

- Improper preparation of the substrate (sanding and cleaning).
- Omitting or applying an incompatible undercoat to a specific substrate (e.g., aluminum, galvanized, plastics).
- Insufficient flash/dry time or exceeding the product's maximum recoat time.
- Insufficient film thickness of undercoat or top coat.
- For clear-coat finishes: (1) insufficient film thickness of clear coat; (2) solvent cleaning base coat before clear coating; (3) sanding base coat before applying additional base coat or clear coat; (4) base coat applied too dry; (5) clear coat applied too dry; (6) baking base coat before applying clear coat; (7) using fisheye eliminator in base coat; (8) incompatible clear coat; (9) use of incompatible "adhesion promoter"; (10) excessive base coat film thickness; (11) overreduction, underreduction, or incompatible reducer used in base coat.

REPAIR

- Remove the finish in the affected area, featheredge, and refinish.
- Or strip to bare substrate and refinish.

PREVENTION

- Clean and prepare all substrates according to product recommendations.
- Use the recommended undercoat (primer) for the substrate being finished. Plastic parts may require use of a special primer and flex additive for maximum performance.
- Recoat all products within their recommended minimum and maximum recoat time.
- Apply a sufficient number of coats to obtain the recommended film thickness.
- Follow base-coat/clear-coat application procedures using only recommended/compatible products.
- "Adhesion promoter" should only be used when specifically recommended.

PINHOLING IN BODY FILLER
(Bubbles, Air Pockets)
Small holes or bubbles located in or on top of putties or body fillers.

CAUSE
Air or gas bubbles become trapped inside putty or filler during mixing or product application. These bubbles are exposed during the sanding process, creating small holes or craters in the surface. Air or gas is trapped when:
- Filler and hardener are mixed together using a "whipping" motion (fast circular motion).
- Too much hardener is added.
- Heavy, thick coats have been applied, producing excessive heat and causing gas bubbles to form inside the product as it cures.

REPAIR
Apply a thin layer of polyester glazing putty (properly catalyzed and mixed), sand smooth, and continue the repair process.

PREVENTION
- Mix putty/filler components by folding together and pressing down to eliminate air pockets.
- Apply putty/filler in thin coats. Do not exceed manufacturer's recommended total film thickness.
- Follow manufacturer's recommendation of correct ratio of putty/filler to hardener.

RUNS/SAGS
(Hangers, Curtains, Signatures)
Coatings that fail to adhere uniformly, causing beads, droplets, or slippage of the total film.

CAUSE
- Overreduction and/or too slow evaporating thinner/reducer.
- Applying paint materials without proper flash time between coats.
- Applying excessively wet coats due to:
(1) Holding the gun too close to the surface.
(2) Slow gun speed.
(3) Double coating.
- Air pressure too low during spray application.
- Improper spray gun setup or an unbalanced spray pattern.
- Material and/or substrate temperature too cold.

REPAIR
- Remove the wet paint film with solvent, clean, and refinish.
- Or, after finish is completely dry, remove excess paint by block sanding with 1,200 or finer grit sandpaper, compound, and polish to restore gloss.
- Or block-sand smooth and refinish.

PREVENTION
- Mix according to product directions. Select recommended solvent for spray conditions based on temperature, humidity, air movement, and size of repair.
- Spray medium wet coats and allow sufficient flash time between coats.
- Adjust the spray gun for the best atomization and balanced spray pattern before paint application. Hold the spray gun perpendicular and parallel to the panel. Adjust speed of pass, pattern overlap, and distance from the panel until the desired results are achieved.
- Set air pressure at the gun according to product recommendations.
- Use recommended spray gun, including fluid tip and air cap combination.
- Allow the paint material and substrate to reach room temperature before application.

SANDING MARKS
(Streaked Finish, Sand Scratches)
Dark and/or streaked marks that resemble sand scratches in the paint film.

CAUSE
Scratching or distorting metallic/mica flakes close to the surface of the paint film due to:
- Sanding single-stage or base-coat metallic finishes prior to clear coating.
- Sanding single-stage metallic finishes prior to buffing.

REPAIR
Allow finish to dry, then sand and refinish.

PREVENTION
- Avoid sanding base-coat finishes before clear coating. If sanding is necessary, apply additional color following label direction.

- When sanding single-stage finishes, confine the sanding to minor imperfections (nib sanding rather than entire panels). For best results, use 1,200 or finer grit sandpaper.

SAND SCRATCHES

(Swelling, Sinking, Shrinkage)

Visible lines or marks in the paint film that follow the direction of the sanding process.

CAUSE

- Sanding the substrate with too-coarse-grit sandpaper.
- Insufficient dry/cure of undercoats before sanding and top coating.
- Refinishing over soft, soluble substrates (e.g., lacquers, uncured OEM).
- Using poor grade and/or too fast evaporating thinners/reducers for spray conditions causing:
(1) Primer surfacer to "bridge" over sand scratches.
(2) Top coat to "skin over," trapping solvent, which swells sensitive substrates.
- Using a solvent cleaner that is too strong for the substrate or using thinner/reducer as a surface cleaner after sanding.

REPAIR

- Allow finish to dry/cure, sand smooth, compound, or polish to restore gloss.
- Or sand and refinish.

PREVENTION

- Sand with recommended grit sandpaper.
- Allow undercoats to thoroughly dry/cure before sanding and top coating.
- Rub a small area of the old finish with a shop towel saturated with lacquer thinner. If the old finish is soluble or undercured, apply appropriate sealer.
- Select recommended thinner/reducer based on temperature, humidity, air movement, and size of repair.
- Avoid "bridging" existing scratches by applying primer surfacer in thin, wet coats, allowing adequate flash time between each coat.
- Use solvent cleaner designated for either lacquer (soluble) or cured enamel/urethane (insoluble) substrates.

SEEDINESS

(Gritty, Dirty, Grainy, Speckled)

Solid particles of various shapes and sizes embedded evenly throughout the paint film.

CAUSE

- Material not properly stirred or agitated.
- Failure to strain material.
- Using material exceeding its shelf life.
- Using generic reducers and/or hardeners.
- Using materials beyond their specified pot life.
- Using contaminated thinner/reducer or hardener.
- Using contaminated waterborne products.

REPAIR

- Remove the wet paint film with solvent, clean, and refinish.
- Or sand smooth and refinish.

PREVENTION

- Stir or shake materials thoroughly to be sure all pigment/resin is in solution.
- Strain all undercoats and top coats.
- Do not use material that cannot be stirred or strained. *Caution: Repeated straining will not completely remove seediness.*
- Use the recommended thinner/reducer and hardener, and then measure accurately.
- Mix only enough material as can be used within specified pot life.
- Use material as soon as possible; close and tighten container lids immediately after use.
- Do not allow thinner/reducer to come into contact with waterborne products.

SHRINKAGE

(Bullseyes, Ringing, Edge Mapping)

The repaired area, featheredge, or sand scratches become visible within hours, days, or weeks after the repair is completed.

CAUSE

- Top coating before undercoats have thoroughly dried/cured.
- Undercoats applied excessively wet with inadequate flash time between coats.
- Undercoats underreduced.

- Using a poor grade and/or too fast evaporating thinner/reducer for spray conditions.
- Finishing over body filler that has not thoroughly cured.
- Using too strong of a solvent cleaner or using thinner/reducer as a surface cleaner.

REPAIR

- Allow the affected area to thoroughly dry/cure; then sand and refinish.
- If additional filling is necessary, apply a primer surfacer, sand smooth, and refinish.

PREVENTION

- Allow undercoats to thoroughly dry/cure before sanding and/or top coating.
- Thin or reduce undercoats according to product label directions. Apply in thin wet coats, allowing adequate flash time between coats to avoid "bridging" scratches.
- Select recommended thinner/reducer based on temperature, humidity, air movement, and size of repair.
- Follow body filler manufacturer's recommended cure time.
- Use solvent cleaner designated for either lacquer soluble or cured enamel/urethane insoluble substrate.

SOFT FILM

(Slow Dry)

The paint film is soft to the touch and will fingerprint or waterspot within hours/days after application.

CAUSE

- Applying undercoat and/or top coat excessively wet.
- Insufficient dry time between coats.
- Improper shop ventilation or heating.
- Adding too much or too little hardener to the paint material.
- Using an incorrect thinner/reducer for spray conditions.
- Omission of drier in enamel/urethane top coats.

REPAIR

- Allow additional dry time, maintaining a shop temperature of 70 degrees Fahrenheit or above.
- Or force dry following temperature and time recommendations.
- Or remove soft paint film and refinish.

PREVENTION

- Use recommended spray gun, fluid tip, and air cap for the material being sprayed. Always adjust the gun for best atomization and balance spray pattern before paint application.
- Allow sufficient flash time between coats.
- Maintain shop temperature at 70 degrees Fahrenheit or above for proper dry/cure.
- Use the recommended hardener and measure accurately.
- Select appropriate thinner/reducer based on temperature, humidity, air movement, and size of repair. Allow additional flash time when spraying in high temperature/high humidity or low temperature/high humidity conditions.
- Add the correct amount of drier that is specifically listed in the color formulation.

SOLVENT POPPING

(Boiling, Blowing)

Small bubbles, pinholes, or craterlike openings in or on the paint film.

CAUSE

Liquid solvent (thinners/reducers) becomes "trapped" in the paint film when the surface layer skins over too quickly, preventing its evaporation into the atmosphere. Solvents that vaporize within the paint film leave bubbles, pinholes, or craters as they push through and "pop" the surface. Solvents can be trapped due to:

- Thinner/reducer evaporating too fast for spraying conditions.
- Inadequate flash time between coats.
- Excessive film thickness or "piling on" of heavy/wet coats.
- Too much air movement causing surface to "skin over" before solvents evaporate.
- Excessive purge/flash time before force drying.

REPAIR

- Allow finish to thoroughly dry/cure, sand smooth, and refinish. Inspect surface carefully to ensure all craters have been removed.
- Severe popping will require removal of the affected film. Prime, seal, and recoat as necessary.

PREVENTION

- Select recommended thinner/reducer based on temperature, humidity, air movement, and size of repair.
- Allow for proper flash time between coats.
- Avoid "piling on" or double wet coats.
- Restrict air movement over the surface being painted.
- Avoid extended purge/flash time before force drying.

Note: Fine dust particles that fall on a tacky surface can be encapsulated by the wet film, creating an appearance almost identical to solvent pop. This "solvent pop" appearance usually occurs on panels or components that are removed from the paint area in a somewhat tacky condition and placed in another location to dry. Fine dust contamination can be removed by sanding and polishing; however, if the condition is solvent pop, the finish will contain pinholes or small craters after being sanded.

STAINING/PLASTIC BLEED-THROUGH
(Discoloration)

A yellow-brown discoloration appears in the top coat over areas repaired with polyester body filler or glazing putty.

CAUSE

- Using too much or too little hardener in the putty/filler.
- Insufficient mixing of putty/filler components.
- Applying a surfacer, sealer, and/or top coat before putty/filler has thoroughly cured.
- Applying undercoats and/or top coats excessively wet.
- Clear coating a white or light color without using a stain-free body filler.

REPAIR

- Allow top coat to thoroughly cure.
- Sand affected area, isolate with two-component undercoats, and refinish.

PREVENTION

- Use correct amount of body filler hardener.
- Mix components thoroughly.
- Allow putty/filler to cure thoroughly before top coating.
- Apply undercoats and/or top coats in medium-wet to wet coats, always allowing proper flash time between coats.
- Use nonstaining body filler, especially when clear coating light colors.
- Isolate suspected staining filler by applying a two-component surfacer and sealer.

- Allow to cure, following product recommendations; then apply desired top coat.
- Two-component acrylic urethane primer surfacer and acrylic urethane sealer may be used to top a majority of body filler staining problems. Both are required and must be allowed to fully cure for maximum stain resistance. For 100 percent assurance against body filler staining, use a nonstaining body filler, following manufacturer's recommendations.

TAPE TRACKING
(Tracks)

An imprinted line or texture in the dried paint film following the use of masking tape.

CAUSE

- The finish is not dry before taping, causing solvent entrapment between finish and tape.
- Using a nonautomotive tape for multicolor finishes. Solvents from additional color soak through the tape and into the previous color.

REPAIR

- Compound and polish to remove texture.
- Or sand with 1,500- to 2,000-grit sandpaper, compound, and polish to restore gloss.
- Or sand and refinish.

PREVENTION

- Allow the finish to thoroughly dry before masking.
- Use only high-quality automotive masking tape.
- Determine if it is safe to tape on freshly painted surfaces by applying a small piece of tape to the surface for 10 to 15 minutes; then remove and check for imprinting.
- Untack the tape before applying by pulling the adhesive side of the tape over your pant leg or between your fingers.
- Remove the tape as quickly as possible after applying additional color(s).

TRANSPARENCY
(Poor Hiding, Poor Coverage, Translucent)

The original finish or undercoat is visible through the top coat.

CAUSE

- The color is not thoroughly stirred/agitated.
- The color is overthinned/reduced.

- Substrate not uniform in color.
- Wrong color undercoat used.
- Insufficient number of color coats applied.

REPAIR
- Apply additional coats of color until hiding is achieved.
- Or sand and apply similar colored undercoat/ground coat and refinish.

PREVENTION
- Stir or shake paint material thoroughly, making sure all pigment is in solution/suspension.
- Thin/reduce according to product label directions.
- Use a sealer or ground coat to provide a uniform color before top coating.
- Use an undercoat that is similar in color to the top coat.
- Spray until hiding is achieved.

Note: Spray monitors (hiding power labels, opacity charts) provide a contrasting feature by which to observe the hiding power or transparency of top-coat color during spray application. When black and white can no longer be seen through the color, complete coverage is achieved.

WATER SPOTTING
(Water Marking)
Circles with raised edges or whitish spots resembling the various shapes of water droplets appear on the surface of the paint film.

CAUSE
- Allowing water to come into contact with a finish that is not thoroughly dried/cured.
- Washing finish in direct sunlight.

REPAIR
- Wipe with a damp cloth, then polish.
- Or compound and polish.
- Or sand smooth with 1,500- to 2,000-grit sandpaper, compound, and polish to restore gloss.
- Or sand and refinish.

PREVENTION
- Do not allow water to come into contact with newly painted finish.
- If a new finish does get wet, dry immediately with a soft cloth.
- Wash new finishes in the shade and wipe dry.

WRINKLING
(Crinkling, Puckering, Shriveling)
The surface of the paint contains irregular grooves or ridges resembling the skin of a prune.

CAUSE
- Excessive film thickness or "piling on" of heavy wet coats.
- Placing a newly painted finish in the hot sun too soon after spraying.
- Using lacquer thinner to reduce synthetic enamel.
- Spraying in extreme hot, humid weather conditions.
- Using underreduced and/or too fast evaporating thinner/reducer for spray conditions.
- Air pressure is too low during spray application.
- Force drying air-dry enamels without the recommended additives.

REPAIR
- If defects are minor, sand the top surface smooth, allow to cure, and refinish.
- If defects are severe, remove the affected area and refinish.

PREVENTION
- Avoid excessive film thickness and heavy coats. Always allow for sufficient flash times.
- Keep newly painted finish away from direct sunlight until finish has dried/cured.
- Use reducer that is specifically recommended for the top coat.
- Use the recommended reducer, additive, and/or retarder when spraying in hot, humid weather.
- Select recommend thinner/reducer based on temperature, humidity, air movement, and size of repair.
- Use the proper reduction ratio and spray at recommended air pressure.
- Select the recommended additives to suit drying conditions. Follow force-dry temperatures and time recommendations.

PARTS AND PAINT SUPPLY SOURCES

Paint Suppliers

(A list of retailers for the automotive paint suppliers, such as Martin-Senour and DuPont, is available on each company's website.)

Akzo Nobel Coatings Inc.
2031 Nelson Miller Parkway
Louisville, KY 40223
502-254-0470
www.akzonobel.com

DuPont
24-hour information in the United States: 1-800-441-7515; Worldwide: 1-302-774-1000
http://www2.dupont.com/
Automotive/en_US/
products_services/paint
Coatings/paintCoatings.
html

PPG World Headquarters
One PPG Place
Pittsburg, PA 15272
412-434-3131
www.corporateportal.ppg.
com/PPG/transportation

Martin-Senour
1-800-526-6704
Technical and color line or contact your local NAPA dealer.
www.martinsenour-autopaint.com

Sherwin-Williams
1-800-4-SHERWIN
(1-800-474-3794)
www.sherwin-automotive.
com

TISCO
1-800-338-0145
Customer Assistance:
Option 1
Technical Assistance:
Option 2
www.tiscoparts.com
Parts, paint, and decals

Tractor Parts Inc.
P.O. Box 2187
Glasgow, KY 42142
270-651-2547
www.tractorpartsinc.com
Parts, paint, and decals

Van Sickle Paint
305 M Street
Lincoln, NE 68501
402-476-6558
www.vansicklepaint.com

Chemical Suppliers

Chlor*Rid International Inc.
P.O. Box 908
Chandler, AZ 85244
1-800-422-3217
480-821-0039
www.chlor-rid.com
*Makers of Chlor*Rid and Chlor*Wash cleaning products*

Eldorado Solutions Inc.
11611 North Meridian Street Suite 600
Carmel, IN 46032
1-800-531-1088 or
317-818-8500
E-mail: techsupport@
eldoradochem.com
www.eldoradochem.com
Maker of DoradoStrip paint stripper

International Chemical Products Inc.
1209 Meadow Park Drive
Huntsville, AL 35803
256-650-0088
E-mail: rsen@cpi.net
www.picklex20.com
Makers of Picklex 20 one-step metal prep

RustGuy Rust Converter
866-787-8489
www.rustguy.com

Parts Sources

DECALS

Lyle Dumont
20545 255th Street
Sigourney, IA 52591
515-622-2592
Decals for Oliver, Hart-Parr, and Massey-Harris

Jorde's Decals
Travis & Shirley Jorde
935 Ninth Avenue NE
Rochester, MN 55906
507-288-5483
www.millcomm.com/-
jorde/index.htm
Decals for John Deere

Kenneth Funfsinn
Route 2
Mendota, IL 61342

K & K Antique Tractors
5995 N. 100 W.
West Shelbyville, IN 46176
317-398-9883
www.kkantiquetractors.
com

Jack Maple
Route 1, Box 154
Rushville, IN 46173
317-932-2027
Decals for a wide variety of applications and models

Keith McClure
12331 County Road 316
Big Prairie, OH 44611
330-567-3951
www.cockshuttdecals.com
Decals for Cockshutt and Co-Op tractors

Dan Shima
409 Sheridan Drive
Eldridge, IA 52748
319-285-9407

R-M Distributors
3693 M Avenue
Vail, IA 51465
712-677-2491
Decals for Minneapolis-Moline

Lyle Wacker
RR 2, Box 87
Osmond, NE 68765
402-582-4874
Decals for Oliver, Hart-Parr, Case, and Massey-Harris

Specialized Parts

The Brillman Company
Box 333
Tatamy, PA 18085
610-252-9828 (7–9 p.m.
Eastern)
www.brillman.com
John Deere parts

**Campbell's Used Tractor
Parts**
4351 Pulaski Highway
Lawrenceburg, TN 38464
931-762-7185
AC & IH tractor parts

Detwilier Sales
S3266 Highway 13 South
Spenser, WI 54479
715-659-4252
Fax: 715-659-3885
*Specializing in John Deere
two-cylinder parts*

**Dennis Carpenter
Ford Tractor
Reproductions**
P. O. Box 26398
Charlotte, NC 28221-6398
704-786-8139
info@dennis-carpenter.
com
*Ford tractor parts and
reproductions*

Dengler Tractor
6687 Shurz Road
Middletown, OH 45042
513-423-4000
513-423-0706
*John Deere two-cylinder
parts*

Doc's Equipment
1020 Gimlet Creek Road
Sparland, IL 61565
309-469-9224: Shop
309-469-3821: Home
*Allis-Chalmers new and
used parts*

Dave Geyer
1251 Rohret Road S.W.
Oxford, IA 52322
319-628-4257
*John Deere two-cylinder
tractor hoods*

Farmersville Equipment
142 E. Farmersville Road
P. O. Box 638
Ephrata, PA 17522
717-354-2150
New and used Oliver parts

Wilbert Kerchner
1107 1st Avenue
Mendota, IL 61342
815-539-6965
*Specializing in M-M
tractors*

John R. Lair
413 L.Q. P Avenue
Canby, MN 56220
507-223-5902
John Deere fenders

**Little Red Tractor
Company**
124 Marion Street
Howells, NE 68641
402-986-1352

Lynch Farms
1624 Alexandria Road
Eaton, OH 45320
937-456-6686
*Oliver, including louvered
engine side panels*

N-Complete
10594 E. 700 N.
Wilkinson, IN 46186
877-342-2086 (orders)
765-785-2309
765-785-2314 (technical
assistance)
www.n-complete.com
*Ford N-Series parts, paint,
and decals*

**Restoration Supply
Company**
96 Mendon Street
Hopedale, MA 01747
1-800-809-9156
resto@tractorpart.com

Rick's Agri-Parts
4511 Silver Road
Wooster, OH 44691
330-264-9720
www.ricksagriparts.com

Rusty Acre
18024 540th Avenue
Austin, MN 55912
507-433-0073
manifold@smig.net
Old Case parts

Salt Lake Mechanical
2969 West 500 South
Salt Lake City, UT 84104
801-978-9399
Specializing in 8N and 9N

**Shepard's 2 Cylinder
Parts, Service & Repair**
John Shepard
E633-1150 Avenue
Downing, WI 54734
715-265-4988

2-Cylinder Diesel Shop
Roger and Dana Marlin
Route 2, Box 241
Conway, MO 65632
417-589-2634

**Zimmerman Oliver-
Cletrac**
1450 Diamond Station
Road
Ephrata, PA 17522
717-738-2573

Salvage and Miscellaneous Parts

Abilene Machine
Mailing Address:
P.O. Box 129
Abilene, KS 67410-0129
Shipping Address:
2150 Daisy Road
Solomon, KS 67480
1-800-255-0337
www.abilenemachine.com

Ag Tractor Supply
Box 276
Stuart, IA 50250
1-800-944-2898 or
515-523-2363

Alderson Tractor
22724 163rd Avenue
Sigourney, IA 52591
641-624-2275

Alexander Tractor Parts
301 Park Street
Winnsboro, TX 75494
903-342-3001
1-800-231-6876
www.alexanders.com

**All Parts International
Inc. (API)**
3215 West Main Avenue
Fargo, ND 58103
701-235-7503
surplus@stpc.com
www.stpc.com

**Alternative Parts Source
Inc.**
7427 Boliver Road
Chittenango, NY 13037
315-687-0074

Arthurs Tractors
Indiana, PA 15701
1-877-254-FORD (3673)
www.arthurstractors.com

Bates Corporation
4917 14th Road
Bourbon, IN 46504
1-800-248-2955

Berkshire Implement Co., Inc.
U.S. 35 North
Box 237
Royal Center, IN 46978

Bob Martin Antique Tractor Parts
5 Ogle Industrial Drive
Vevay, IN 47043
812-427-2622
www.venus.net~martin

Biewer's Tractor and Restoration Salvage
16242 140th Avenue South
Barnesville, MN 56514
218-493-4696
bts@rrt.net
www.salvagetractors.com

Carter & Gruenewald Co., Inc
4414 Hwy 92
P. O. Box 40
Brooklyn, WI 53521
608-455-2411
cngcoinc@mailbag.com
www.cngco.com

CT Farm & Country
Box 3330
Des Moines, IA 50316
1-800-247-7508 (General)
1-800-247-0128 (Used)

Central Michigan Tractor & Parts
2713 N. U.S. 27
St. Johns, MI 48879
1-800-248-9263

Central Plains Tractor Parts
712 North Main Avenue
Sioux Falls, SD 57102
1-800-234-1968
605-334-0021

Colfax Tractor Parts
Route 1, Box 119
Colfax, IA 50054
1-800-284-3001

Dave Cook
R.R. 1, Box 25
Washburn, WI 54891
715-373-2092

Dick Moore Repair & Salvage
1540 Joe Quick Road
New Market, AL 35761
205-828-3884

Discount Tractor Supply
Box 265
Franklin Grove, IL 61031
1-800-433-5805

Draper Tractor Parts
1951 Draper-Brown Road
Garfield, WA 99130
1-800-967-8185
509-397-2666

Dave Geyer
1251 Rohret Road S.W.
Oxford, IA 52322
319-628-4257

Ellis County Tractor
1513 E. Main
Waxahachie, TX 75165
972-923-0401

Faust Bros. Repair
26768 193rd Street
Pierz, MN 56364
320-468-6051

Fresno Tractor Parts
3444 West Whitesbridge Road
Fresno, CA 93706
209-233-2174

Heritage Farm Power Inc.
P. O. Box 1125
Belton, MO 64012
816-322-1898
www.tractorumbrellas.com
Vintage tractor umbrellas

Iowa Falls Tractor Parts
Route 3, Box 330A
Iowa Falls, IA 50126
1-800-232-3276

Norman Jackson
5013 E. 100 S.
Greenfield, IN 46140
317-431-4803 (cell)

J. P. Tractor Salvage
1347 Madison 426
Fredericktown, MO 63645
573-783-7055
parts@jptractorsalvage.com
www.jptractorsalvage.com

Klumpp Salvage
Highway 165 South
Kinder, LA 70648
1-800-444-8038
318-738-2554

John R. Lair
413 L.Q. P. Ave.
Canby, MN 56220
507-223-5902
Fenders

Mark's Tractors
2636 County Road 2300 E.
Gifford, IL 61847
217-694-4735

Martin's Farm Supply
5 Ogle Industrial Drive
Vevay, IN 47043
812-427-2622
www.antiquetractorparts.com
New and used parts

Mathis Equipment and Tractor Salvage
P. O. Box 79
Cairo, MO 65239
660-295-4456

Novotny Repair
2631 320th Street
Chelsea, IA 52215
641-489-2271 or 641-489-2070
New and used parts

O.E.M. Tractor Parts
Route 9 East
P.O. Box 362
Bloomington, IL 61702
1-800-283-2122
www.oemtractorparts.com

Parts of the Past Inc.
1320 Spencer Drive
Lawrence, KS 66044
785-749-5231
Many new old stock (NOS) parts

Pete's Tractor Salvage Inc.
2163 15th Avenue NE
Anamoose, ND 58710
1-800-541-7383
701-465-3274

PDQ Parts
Box 71007
Des Moines, IA 50322
1-800-274-7334
515-254-0014

Phil's Tractor & Supply Inc.
925 Applegate Road
Madison, WI 53713
608-274-3601
www.philstractor.com

Harold Robinson
R.R. 1, Box 161
Queen City, MO 63561
660-766-2762
(5:30 p.m.–9:30 p.m.
Mon–Sat. only)
hrrobih@marktwain.net

Smith Tractor
898 Highway 25 N.
Travelers Rest, SC 29690
864-834-3009

South-Central Tractor Parts
Route 1, Box 1
Leland, MS 38756
1-800-247-1237

Southeast Tractor Parts
Route 2, Box 565
Jefferson, SC 29718
1-888-658-7171

Steiner Tractor Parts Inc.
P.O. Box 449
Lennon, MI 48449
1-800-234-3280
sales@steinertractor.com
www.steinertractor.com

Surplus Tractor Parts Corporation
Box 2125
Fargo, ND 58107
1-800-859-2045
701-235-7503

Taylor Equipment
3694-2 Mile Road
Sears, MI 49679
1-800-368-3276
231-734-5213
Fax: 231-734-3113

TTP Inc.
3114 East U.S. Highway 30
Warsaw, IN 46580
1-800-825-7711

The Tractor Barn
West Highway 60
Brookline, MO 65619
1-800-383-3678
417-881-3668

TractorHouse.Com
P. O. Box 85670
Lincoln, NE 68501
1-800-307-5199
402-479-2154
www.tractorhouse.com

Tractor Parts Unlimited
24755 Highway 12 East
Ethel, MS 39067
866-996-7278
www.tractorparts
unlimited.com

Tractor Works
10207 N. County Road 300 W.
Jamestown, IN 46147
765-676-6292

Thorne Farm Equipment
Box 358
Chesnee, SC 29323
803-461-7719

Tired Iron Farm
19467 County Road 8
Bristol, IN 46507
574-848-4628

Van Noort Tractor Salvage
1003 10th Avenue
Rock Valley, IA 51247
1-800-831-4814

Walthill Service and Supply
P.O. Box 2B
103 N. Tallman
Walthill, NE 68067
402-846-5450

Watertown Tractor Parts
2510 9th Avenue S.W.
Watertown, SD 57201
1-800-843-4413

Watson Farm Equipment and Tractor Parts
Route 2
Ariss, Ontario, Canada N0B1B0
519-846-5279
519-846-0776 (Parts)

Weber's Tractor Works
201 S. Lafayette
Newton, IL 62448
618-783-4102 (IL)
507-434-0876 (MN)
wtw@weberstractorworks.com
www.ihparts.com
Many new old stock (NOS) parts

Wengers of Myerstown
814 South College Street
Myerstown, PA 17067
1-800-451-5240
717-866-2135
www.wengers.com

Wilson Tractor Parts
12th and Main Streets
N. Little Rock, AR 72201
501-372-7374
www.tractorshack.com

Worthington Tractor Salvage
Route 4, Box 14
Worthington, MN 56187
1-800-533-5304

Yesterday's Tractors
P. O. Box 160
Chicacum, WA 98325
www.ytmag.com

GAUGES

Antique Gauges Inc.
12287 Old Skipton Road
Cordova, MD 21625
410-822-4963

STEERING WHEELS— RECOVERING

Tom Lein
24185 Denmark Avenue
Farmington, MN 55024
651-463-2141

Minn-Kota Repair
R.R. 1, Box 243
Ortonville, MN 56278
320-839-3940 or
320-289-2473

Tractor Steering Wheel Recovering and Repair
1400 121st Street W
Rosemount, MN 55068
612-455-1802

SEATS

Silver Seats
Darrel Darst
1857 West Outer Highway 61
Moscow Mills, MO 63362
636-356-4764 (nights)
636-528-4877, ext. 113 (days)

Speer Cushion Company
431 S. Interocean Avenue
Holyoke, CO 80734
1-800-525-8156
970-854-2911
E-mail: spearcushion@ pctelcom.coop
www.speercushion.com

TIRES

M. E. Miller Tire Co.
17386 State Highway 2
Wauseon, OH 43567
1-800-621-1955 Ext. 4
419-335-7010
www.millertire.com

Tucker's Tire
844 S. Main Street
Dyersburg, TN 38024
1-800-443-0802

RESTORATION EQUIPMENT AND MATERIALS

CJ Spray Inc.
370 Airport Road
South St. Paul, MN 55075
1-800-328-4827
Spray systems

Jim Deardorff
Box 317
Chillicothe, MO 64601
660-646-6355
Fax: 660-646-3329
jdeardorff@yahoo.com
Classic Blast sandblasting mix and equipment

TP Tools and Equipment
Dept. AP, 7075 Route 446,
P.O. Box 649
Canfield, OH 44406
1-800-321-9260
Info line: 330-533-3384
www.tiptools.com
Parts washers, grinders, presses, sandblasting equipment

Restoration Services

Anderson Tractors
Route 3, Box 632
Webster, SD 57274
712-382-1877

Fletcher's Garage
32624 Route 11
Modesto, IL 62667
217-439-7400

John J. Hill
221 Atkinson Drive
Millington, MD 21651
410-928-3774
410-725-6338

Marks Tractor Painting and Parts
2636 County Road 2300 E.
Gifford, IL 61847
217-694-4735

Midwest Tractor Restoration
Waverly, MN
612-232-1876

P & R Repair
1432 M Avenue
Perry, IA 50220
515-676-2215
Professional antique tractor restorations

Uken Tractor Restoration
1909 330th Street
Titonka, IA 50480
515-928-2010
ukentr@netins.net
Specializing in John Deere two-cylinder

Valentine Specialties
P. O. Box 120
208 E. Street N
Laurens, IA 50554
712-841-2650
Specializing in IH restoration

Nichols Restorations
484 E. State St.
Presqueisle, ME 04769
207-762-8005
deere@maine.rr.com
www.homestead.com/tknichols/troyjd.html

7 Oaks Restoration and Supply
45 Westwood Avenue
Scarborough, ME 04074
207-883-1689
7oaks@maine.rr.com

Ken's Body Shop
Huron, OH 44839
1-800-843-2395

Joe's Auto Body
11807 Lax Chapel Road
Kiel, WI 53042
920-894-2134
joesautobody@excel.net

Proctor Antique Restoration & Refinishing
854 State Highway E
Benton, MO 63736
573-450-2704
573-545-3226

Miller Equipment Transfer & Repair
1348 St. Luke Road
Woodstock, VA 22664
540-459-7477

Publications & Clubs

TRACTOR MANUALS

Binder Books
27875 SW Grahams Ferry Road
Sherwood, OR 97140
503-684-2024
www.binderbooks.com

Clarence L. Goodburn Literature Sales
101 W. Main
Madelia, MN 56062
507-642-3281

Jensales Inc.
P.O. Box 277
Clarks Grove, MN 56016
1-800-443-0625 (orders)
507-826-3666
www.jensales.com

Intertec Publishing
P. O. Box 12901
Overland Park, KS 66282
1-800-262-1954
www.intertecbooks.com

King's Books
P.O. Box 86
Radnor, OH 43066

Yesterday's Tractors
P.O. Box 160
Chicacum, WA 98325
www.ytmag.com

GENERAL MAGAZINES/ CLUBS

Antique Power
P.O. Box 838
Yellow Springs, OH 45387
1-800-767-5828
E-mail: antique@antique power.com
www.antiquepower.com

The Belt Pulley
P.O. Box 58
Jefferson, WI 53549
920-674-9732
E-mail: info@beltpulley.com
www.beltpulley.com

The Hook Magazine
P.O. Box 16
Marshfield, MO 65706
417-468-7000
Tractor pulling, including

antique and classic
Vintage Garden Tractor Club of America
412 W. Chestnut
Pardeeville, WI 53954
608-429-4520
E-mail: towrpowr27@yahoo.com
www.vgtacoa.com

CLUBS AND BRAND NEWSLETTERS/ MAGAZINES

Advance-Rumely
The Rumley Newsletter
P.O. Box 12
Moline, IL 61265
309-764-7653

Rumley Collectors News
12109 Mennonite Church Road
Tremont, IL 61568
309-925-3925

ALLIS-CHALMERS

The Allis Connection
4610 South Curtiss Road
Stockton, IL 61085
815-947-9881
allisacres@blakhawk.net

Old Allis News
10925 Love Road
Bellevue, MI 49021
269-763-9770
allisnews@aol.com

B. F. AVERY

B. F. Avery Collectors Newsletter
14651 S. Edon Road
Camden, MI 49232
517-368-5595

CASE

J. I. Case Collectors' Association
P.O. Box 638
Beecher, IL 60401
Trailsend1@aol.com

J. I. Case Heritage
Foundation
Office of the Secretary
P. O. Box 081156
Racine, WI 53408

CATERPILLAR

**Antique Caterpillar
Machinery**
Owners Club and
Newsletter
7501 N. University
Suite 119
Peoria, IL 61614
www.acmoc.org

COCKSHUTT

**International Cockshutt
Club**
1506 Indian Lakes Road
Kent City, MI 49330
616-887-7462

EMPIRE

**Empire Tractor
Newsletter**
5862 State Route 90 N.
Cayuga, NY 13034
315-253-8151
E-mail: info@empire
tractor.net
www.empiretractor.net

FORD/FORDSON

Ferguson Furrows
1811 Parkway Drive
Bettendorf, IA 52722
E-mail: johniwen@yahoo.
com
www.fergusonenthusiasts.
com

**Ford/Fordson Collectors
Association**
F/FCA Newsletter
645 Loveland-Miamiville
Road
Loveland, OH 45140

Henry Ford's Dreams
C/O Cecil King
R.R. 2
Milton, Ontario, Canada
L9T 2X6

The N-Newsletter
P.O. Box 275
East Corinth, VT 05040-
0275
E-mail: infon@n-news.
com
www.n-news.com

GIBSON

Gibson Tractor Club
ADEHI News (newsletter)
4200 Winwood Court
Floyds Knob, IN 47119-
9225
312-923-5822

INTERNATIONAL
HARVESTER/FARMALL

**IH Collectors Club
Worldwide**
Membership Department
310 Busse Highway, PMB
250
Park Ridge, IL 60068
847-823-8612
www.ihcollectors.org

Red Power Magazine
Box 245
Ida Grove, IA 51445
712-365-2131
www.redpowermagazine.
com

JOHN DEERE

Green Magazine
2652 Davey Road
Bee, NE 68314
402-643-6269
E-mail: info@green
magazine.com
www.greenmagazine.com

**Two-Cylinder Club/
Publications**
P.O. Box 430
Grundy Center, IA 50638-
0010
319-345-2662
E-mail: memberservices@
two-cylinder.com
www.two-cylinder.com

MASSEY-HARRIS

Friends of Massey Inc.
Massey & Related Families
Collectors Club
144 Sherbondy Road
Jamestown, PA 16134
724-932-5424
E-mail: klmlc@wind
stream.net

**Massey-Harris/Ferguson
Collectors**
6130 Guelphline, R.R. 2
Milton, Ontario, Canada
L9T 2X6
E-mail: dgperry@iprimus.
ca

MCA Newsletter
P.O. Box 858
Belton, MO 64012
816-331-5525

MINNEAPOLIS-MOLINE

The Prairie Gold Rush
17390 S. State Road 58
Seymour, IN 47274
812-342-3608
E-mail: prairiegold@
bcremc.net

The M-M Corresponder
3693 M Avenue
Vail, IA 51465
712-677-2491
www.minneapolismoline
collectors.org

OLIVER/HART-PARR

**Hart-Parr Oliver
Collectors Assn.**
11326 N. Parma Road
Springport, MI 49284
517-857-4042
E-mail: becky@hartparr
oliver.org
www.hartparroliver.org

Oliver Heritage
P.O. Box 70
Nokomis, IL 62075
217-563-8327
www.oliverinformation.
com

SILVER KING

Silver Kings of Yesteryear
4520 Bullhead Road
Willard, OH 44890
419-935-5842

Information
Resources

Spray Gun World
http://www.spraygun
world.com/Information2/
Help.htm
Paint spraying and gun
care videos, Q & A, etc.

**Wisconsin Historical
Society**
McCormick-IHC
Collection
816 State Street
Madison, WI 53706
lcgrady@whs.wisc.edu
www.wisconsinhistory.org/
libraryacrchives/ihc

INDEX

ABOUT THE AUTHOR

Tharran E. Gaines was born in north-central Kansas, where he grew up as the only boy in a family of five children on a small grain and livestock farm near the town of Kensington. He attended Kansas State University, where he received a degree in wildlife conservation and journalism with the goal of pursuing outdoor writing. Instead, he was soon using his agricultural background as a technical writer for Hesston Corporation and hasn't left agriculture since.

As a technical writer, he has produced repair manuals, owner's manuals, and assembly instructions for companies that include Hesston, Winnebago, Sundstrand, Kinze, and Best Way. As a creative writer, he has crafted and produced everything from newsletter and feature articles to radio and TV commercials and video scripts and advertising copy for such companies as DeKalb Seed Company, DowElanco, Asgrow Seed Company, Farmland Industries, Caterpillar, Challenger, Gleaner, Massey Ferguson, and T-L Irrigation.

In 1991, after working for various corporations and advertising agencies, he began his own business as a freelance writer and today continues to operate Gaines Communications with his wife, Barb, out of their home office. The majority of their business involves producing editorial and advertising copy for agricultural clients involved in the farm machinery industry and working with Voyageur Press on a series of classic tractor restoration books.

Tharran and his wife live in a 130-plus-year-old Victorian home in Savannah, Missouri.